The Autobiography
of a Slave

Autobiografía de
un esclavo

LATIN AMERICAN LITERATURE AND CULTURE SERIES

Books in this series

Violent Acts: A Study of Violence in Contemporary Latin American Theatre, by Severino João Albuquerque, 1991

Feminist Perspectives on Sor Juana Inés de la Cruz, edited by Stephanie Merrim, 1991

The Impenetrable Madam X, by Griselda Gambaro, translated by Evelyn Picon Garfield, 1991

Autor/lector: Huidobro, Borges, Fuentes y Sarduy, by Alicia Rivero-Potter, 1991

José Donoso's House of Fiction: A Dramatic Construction of Time and Place, by Flora González Mandri, 1995

The Autobiography of a Slave / Autobiografía de un esclavo, by Juan Francisco Manzano, introduction and modernized Spanish version by Ivan A. Schulman, English translation by Evelyn Picon Garfield, 1995

The Autobiography of a Slave

Autobiografía de un esclavo

by Juan Francisco Manzano

A Bilingual Edition

Introduction and
Modernized Spanish Version
by Ivan A. Schulman

Translated by Evelyn Picon Garfield

 Wayne State University Press
Detroit

Library of Congress Cataloging-in-Publication Data

Manzano, Juan Francisco, 1797–1854
    The autobiography of a slave / by Juan Francisco Manzano ; introduction
and modernized Spanish version by Ivan A. Schulman ; translated by Evelyn
Picon Garfield = Autobiografía de un esclavo. — Bilingual ed.
        p. cm. — (Latin American literature and culture series)
    Includes bibliographical references.
    ISBN 0-8143-2537-8 (alk. paper). — ISBN 0-8143-2538-6 (pbk. : alk.
paper)
    1. Manzano, Juan Francisco, 1797–1854. 2. Slaves—Cuba—Biography.
I. Title. II. Series.
HT1076.M2813   1996
305.5'67'092—dc20
[B]   95-25853

Grateful acknowledgment is made to the University of Illinois Research
Board for its support during the preparation of this book and to Paul Eric
Henager for his assistance with the translation portion of the manuscript.

Introduction

Ivan A. Schulman

Yearning for Liberty

"A slave is a dead soul,"[1] wrote Juan Francisco Manzano. In his *Autobiography*, this Cuban Creole mulatto recounts the tormented existence of an urban slave in the mid-1800s. It is a tragic narrative that brought tears to the eyes of the few contemporaries who read it in Cuba, where censorship under a colonial regime precluded its publication.[2] However, in England, where it was published almost immediately upon its completion, it was regarded as a documentary account that lay bare the horrors of slavery and gave credence to the English abolitionist's militant campaign for terminating this nefarious form of human exploitation in the Caribbean.

Manzano was a slave in the "master" house, for which reason his situation was considered "privileged" on a scale of degradations whose calibrations Alexander Humboldt interpreted in his *Political Essay on the Island of Cuba:*

> What a distance between the slave who serves in the house of a wealthy man in Havana and in Kingston, and one who works for himself, giving to his master a daily sum, and the slave who works on a sugar plantation! The threats that are used to correct a recalcitrant African provide insight into this scale of human privation. The carriage driver is threatened with the coffee plantation, the slave who labors in the coffee plantation, with the sugar fields. The sugar-mill slave who has a wife, who lives in a separate house, who with

the affection that characterizes most of the Africans, finds after a day's work someone to care for him, in the midst of an indigent family, has a fate that cannot be compared to that of a slave who is isolated and lost in the crowd. This diversity of rank is unknown to those who have not witnessed slavery in the Antilles. The progressive improvement of station, even within the ranks of slavery, makes it possible to understand how, in Cuba, the wealth of the master and the possibility of earnings from labor have been able to attract more than 80,000 slaves to the cities, how manumission favored by the wisdom of the law has been sufficiently active to have produced, without going beyond current times, more than 130,000 free persons of color.[3]

To belong to the ranks of these free persons of color was Manzano's most cherished desire; in fact, it was the most tenacious and energetic driving force of his life, as we shall see in the painful narrative of his *Autobiography*—the only account written by a Cuban slave prior to the official abolition of slavery on the island in 1886. His life, if one only takes into account physical pain, was undoubtedly more fortunate than that of other Africans—those, for example, who labored long hours under the tropical sun in the sugarcane fields. But mental anguish and torment, like physical punishment—which Manzano also suffered—created wounds and left scars that marked the young slave for the rest of his life. In bondage he constantly dreamed of his ransom,[4] that is, the price of his freedom, which neither his literary talent nor his refined manners in and by themselves could bring him. He was a slave, and as such he suffered the lot of all slaves, including the "disastrous moral consequences"[5] that branded both masters and slaves.

The period of Cuban history to which the *Autobiography* belongs was one in which the island's wealth depended principally on the production of sugar and, to a lesser degree, coffee.[6] And up to the end of the first half of the nineteenth century Cuba's economy depended on slave labor for its prosperity. Treaties had been signed by the Spanish Crown early in the century to ban the importation of slaves, but these agreements were blatantly disregarded by Cuban colonial authorities,

plantation owners, and merchants. The wealth obtained by the cultivation of sugar reached what Hugh Thomas describes as "lavish proportions," and the island's "opulence created a magnificent if somewhat demoralized society. Money seems often to have been treated as a kind of miracle or incitement to spending and dissipation."[7] In his account of his life as a slave, Manzano provides us with a window on all of these historical and economic circumstances.

Many are the histories and chronicles that describe slavery in Cuba;[8] but there are few personal accounts. In contrast with the numerous U.S. slave narratives, in Latin America the personal histories or autobiographies of slaves or former slaves are rare. In fact, Manzano's narrative is the only autobiographical account written by a slave during slavery that has surfaced to date. In Cuba, histories of those who bore the ignominious yoke of human bondage, were in some way connected to the traffic and sale of slaves, or hunted down maroons[9] for their bounty, are extremely limited for reasons both diverse and obvious: first and foremost, the racial and social prejudices of the colonial period's master discourse, which dissuaded writers from representing marginalized peoples or the theme of slavery in their texts; the slaves' almost total illiteracy, which precluded their chronicling the crimes and abuses of slavery; the lack of a clearly developed sense of nationalism, which might have created an interest in preserving the experiences of the slaves through oral histories; and finally, the slaves' constant fear of punishment and the writers' dread of official censorship. As Pedro Deschamps Chapeaux points out, it was no mean feat "to chronicle a marginalized social group within a broader context, when it [the group] is only looked upon as a workforce producing wealth that is appropriated by the masters. Such was the case of the black slave or the freed black within a slave society, in which the voices of protest, rebellion, the constant yearning for liberty were, if not unknown, silenced and subjected to the whip and prison. Those who wrote history were unacquainted with the people who formed part of this history."[10]

The social and economic prejudices that marginalized and suppressed the history of social groups "without history"— principally Chinese and Africans of Cuba—reigned during the

colonial period, and even in the twentieth century they continued to mark the cultural patterns of the "false republic" of the
independent period following the Spanish-American War. Sam-
plings of the testimony of nineteenth-century witnesses, rather
than the discourse of contemporary fictive narratives,[11] substanti-
ate Deschamps's thesis of marginalization. Antonio de las Barras
y Prado, for example, a Spanish merchant from Asturias residing
in Havana and an apologist for slavery, contradicted fictional
depictions of slavery. In his memoirs of 1852 he wrote, "The
sense of horror that Europeans have of slavery is lost here [in
Cuba] because the treatment given to slaves, except in rare cases,
is *not as severe as it is presented in novels*. Many proletarians of free
countries like England would wish to have the treatment of the
slaves of Cuba. It should not be forgotten that my observations
are limited to Havana and its environs" (emphasis added).[12]

To counteract this and other similarly distorted views
of history and in their place provide a more reasoned concept
of national history, twentieth-century Cuban intellectuals have
focused on neglected aspects of the island's cultural and historical development. In his essay "Hacia una nueva historia de
Cuba" (Toward a New History of Cuba), written shortly after
the triumph of the Cuban Revolution, José Antonio Portuondo
observed that "until now [1963], there was no history among
us that did not study the rise and fall of the dominant hegemonic class: the island bourgeoisie." To broaden the recounting of history, he recommended the incorporation into Cuban
historiography of "the exploited classes and . . . their constant
struggles—rebellions of slaves and of free workers, workers' orga-
nizations, strikes . . ."[13]

What writers and intellectuals of the twentieth century
began to demand, particularly following the Cuban Revolution,
was a reconstruction of the island's historical and cultural pro-
cesses as part of a search for authentic roots. In literature it gave
rise to the "non-fictional novel" or "testimonial narrative," whose
principal objective was to discover or uncover the "history of
people without history":

> Up to now the writing of history has been a unilat-
> eral act in which only the voice of the historian was

heard. . . . No matter how careful the historian was to avoid official history, his narrations could not escape the stamp of official accounts. The voices of the common people were drowned out by a supertranscendentalism that summed up their lives in models, sketches, structures. Demographic, ethnological, and sociological studies have enriched the historian's sources and effected a labor of recovery. With the history of the people without history, a new phase, a choral phase, in historical studies commences.[14]

Miguel Barnet's *Biografía de un cimarrón* (Autobiography of a Runaway Slave) (1968) belongs to this new phase. This work is closely connected to Manzano's and invites comparison with it. Barnet narrates the experiences of a centenarian, a former slave who witnessed revolutions and wars; his recollections, recorded on tape in response to Barnet's questions, constitute the individual voice of a collective experience that covers the period from the slave barracks to life in independent Cuba. It is a "choral" work in more than one sense: the protagonist not only relates experiences that belong to the "unknown" history to which Portuondo refers but also collaborates with Barnet, who stimulates his memory with questions whose answers form a national narration. Esteban Montejo, Barnet's protagonist and informant, was first a slave, then a maroon, then a fighter for freedom, and finally a salaried free person. What is of particular interest to us in connection with Manzano's text is that Montejo at a very young age made the decision to abandon his life of servitude forever: "I felt within me the overwhelming spirit of the maroon, from which I could not escape."[15]

The desire to be free was also a consuming force for Manzano, but, unlike Montejo, he was indecisive up to the very last moment about breaking free from his bonds. Montejo and Manzano were two diametrically opposed personalities; their differences not only illustrate how slavery had diverse effects on individual personalities but reveal a great deal about slave psychology—both the master's and the slave's. Montejo is daring and enterprising; Manzano is timid, withdrawn, fearful. But in comparing the two we need to remember that Manzano wrote

about his life while he was still a slave, whereas Montejo, long after slavery had terminated, relates a past nightmare from which he had already been released. Montejo's recounting of the experience of slavery never acquires the heartrending, pathetic quality of Manzano's somber narration, in which a child/adolescent prodigy relates how he frequently was a victim of mortifying, unjust punishments that served to constantly remind him he was, after all, *not* a privileged slave, as he had been brought up to believe, but a social being his society considered inferior. By way of contrast, Montejo focuses on his escape from bondage to the hills where he lived many years in utter isolation. His narrative is of events in the past, spoken from the past, and this allows for a psychological distancing that objectifies and at the same time mollifies the horrors of punishment: "I saw many horrors of punishment under slavery. That's why I didn't like that life. In the boiler house there were the stocks, which were the most cruel. There were stocks for lying down and for standing. They had wide slabs with holes through which they made the slave place his feet, hands, and head. They had them [the slaves] immobilized thus two or three months for some insignificant mistake."[16]

Montejo's "I saw" captures, in a retrospective mode, the suffering of others, and in that sense it depersonalizes the experience of slavery by means of narrative placement and psychological distance. Manzano's account, on the other hand, is a narration of his own daily torment at the hands of fickle authoritarian figures. Montejo, through Barnet, presents the reader with a portrait of a cautious, perspicacious, sometimes humble, but generally enterprising individual who, in the face of successive historical stages of his life, observes that "everything had turned upside down."[17] He does not always fully comprehend the circumstances of his situation—"there are things about life I can't understand"[18]—but his commentaries on a broad spectrum of personal and social issues are sharp and reveal extraordinary insight. His advanced age and his sense of triumph in the face of both chaos and adversity lend a note of optimism and personal achievement to his memoirs.

The social frame of Manzano's text is more limited with respect to both chronology and experience; it narrates the misfortunes and reversals of the slave as a child and a young man.

Insecurity, instability, and injustice are his existential emblems. Unlike Montejo, he is a slave rather than a free man; he fears the vengeance of his perfidious and arbitrary mistress. Hence the silences and voids of his memoirs.

To fully understand this autobiography, we need to keep in mind that the narrator's is a reluctant voice. R. R. Madden (to whom we owe the first, albeit incomplete, edition of the *Autobiography*) says, "the sense of the writer [is] (purposely obscured in the original)."[19] Manzano's fears, given that he was still a slave, undoubtedly caused him, on the one hand, to exaggerate, and, on the other, to delete the presentation of circumstances that might make him or his family vulnerable. There are moments when one has the sense that the slave, his will annihilated by his bondage, identifies with and even shows affection for his sadistic mistress. In evaluating the nature of his slave discourse, the force of the master discourse—that of the hegemonic white oligarchy, Creole or Spanish—is paramount.

Unlike Montejo, Manzano yearned to identify with the dominant white culture, whereas Montejo defended his African heritage with pride, even rejecting the supposed superior wisdom of whites: "There are those—he affirms—that say the African slaves . . . behaved like animals. There's more than one whitey out there who'll say so. . . . They were no savages. Without knowing how to read or write, they taught me many things. Habits are more important than knowledge. To be polite, not to meddle in other's affairs, to speak softly, to respect, be religious, work hard . . . all of this the African slaves taught me."[20]

In Manzano's work we find moments of rebellion and independence, both of which are hallmarks of Montejo's life. However, what predominates in Manzano's self-portrait is the desire to achieve freedom and thus participate fully in the dominant (white) society. To make the leap to the "master" culture was not an uncommon aspiration in the nineteenth century: "Among people of color there existed the general wish to whiten one's descendants insofar as possible, and distance themselves as much as possible from slavery." In so doing, African roots were rejected or trivialized; a sense of one's own worth was sacrificed in favor of a xenophobic ideology. "The popular refrain 'better to be the lover of a white man than the wife of a black man' symbolizes this

conformity, although there were some members of the 'colored class' who rejected it, developing a sort of counter-ideology."[21]

Cintio Vitier notes that Manzano was an "absolute victim,"[22] not merely of slavery but of a concept fostered by the prevailing "white ideology" of not valuing one's African roots. Manzano, as he reveals himself in his *Autobiography* and his letters, seemed not to grasp the limitations colonial society placed on members of his class and race; he was convinced that, given his intellectual gifts, he could, upon realizing his freedom, take his place in the hegemonic "white" social order as an equal. And since achieving liberty was his prime objective, in his *Autobiography* his past is obliterated by his intolerable present. In short, the constructed subject is divorced from ethnic roots and even the most rudimentary notion of cultural or racial identity. The tribulations of the present are foregrounded against a backdrop of the horrors of his mistreatment. The resulting portrait illuminates the slave's search for self-realization; and in the process we gain some insight into the complexities and contradictions of his psychological makeup. The anomalies of the latter may lead readers to reflect on which details of his life Manzano has chosen to highlight and which he has preferred to consign to oblivion. And why, since this is the autobiography of a poet, he does not treat, except in a perfunctory fashion, his creative life, focusing instead on his narrated succession of imprisonments, whippings, and afflictions. Had he concentrated on his development as a writer he might very well have shielded both his person and his family from revealing the daily ordeals he considered a source of embarrassment and shame. Was he instructed to concentrate on the unjust punishments, which were, according to his narrative, his daily lot?

Chronologies

In Manzano's biography there are three key dates: those of his birth, of his manumission, and of the composition of the *Autobiography*. The three, however, are somewhat cloudy if not contradictory, a reflection to be sure of the precarious nature of his existence and the notion that slavery was tantamount to silence, nonexistence, the eradication of historical or individual

consciousness—in short, death. We have excluded his date of death from the discussion of the three key moments of his life simply because prior to the end of his days the poet underwent an enigmatic crisis that caused his premature silence as a writer and poet.

In his *Autobiography* Manzano does not provide his date of birth. José Luciano Franco places Manzano's birth in August of 1797.[23] But in *Cuba poética*, José Fornaris and Joaquín Lorenzo Luaces claim it was 1806 or 1807. And Francisco Calcagno (1829–1903), in *Poetas de color*, contradicts these dates and instead says Manzano was born in 1797, "because that year coincides with the birth of Don Nicolás de Cárdenas, a fact presented by the slave, who writes that between the birth of his young master and his there was no more than a difference of a few days."[24] However, Calcagno, in his *Diccionario biográfico cubano*,[25] gives 1793 as the birth date of Cárdenas. And to complicate matters further, R. R. Madden, in the prologue to the first edition of the *Autobiography* (1840), wrote, "Now he is forty-two years old,"[26] which would mean Manzano was born between 1797 and 1798.

Manzano's freedom—the second key event of his life—is tied to Domingo Del Monte (1804–53), a wealthy intellectual leader and patriot who, like Andrés Bello in Chile, mentored a generation of young writers. Del Monte took a special interest in the poet-slave, for which we are indebted for several reasons. First, he discovered his talent and presented him at his literary gatherings in Matanzas, where during a memorable evening in 1836 Manzano read his sonnet "Thirty Years"[27] before a group of privileged Creoles:

> When I think on the course I have run,
> From my childhood itself to this day,
> I tremble, and fain would I shun
> The remembrance its terrors array.
>
> I marvel at struggles endured,
> With a destiny frightful as mine,
> At the strength for such efforts:—assured
> Tho' I am, 'tis in vain to repine.

I have known this sad life thirty years,
And to me, thirty years it has been[28]
Of suff'ring, of sorrow and tears,
Ev'ry day of its bondage I've seen.

But 'tis nothing the past—or the pains,
Hitherto I have struggled to bear,
When I think, oh, my God! on the chains,
That I know I'm yet destined to wear.

Following the reading of this poem, Del Monte organized a collection that ultimately brought in eight hundred pesos, sufficient to purchase Manzano's freedom. Franco gives 1837 as the date of the poet's freedom,[29] but Cintio Vitier reproduces a letter from Del Monte, dated 23 July 1836, addressed to José Luis Alfonso, Marquis of Montelo,[30] which establishes 1836 as the date of Manzano's liberation. In the letter, Del Monte advises the marquis that Pancho Céspedes, a neighbor,

> will deliver, together with this letter, a tin that contains slices of a most delicious citron prepared by none other than our freed poet, Juan Francisco Manzano, no less accomplished as a confectioner than as a poet. With regard to Manzano, the eight hundred pesos were finally collected, and Pepe de la Luz and I went in person to turn over the "ransom" to Doña María de Zayas. The latter became furious because of the unheard-of ingratitude of that dog of a slave, and considered it an act of insolence to deprive her of a such a servant, after she had gone to such trouble to acquire and train him. He left that house immediately, has set himself up as a confectioner, and is enjoying success, for his confections have caught on. I tell you all this because I know that you will take no small satisfaction in this because of your generous contribution to his liberation.

Following his servitude, as a free black Manzano exercised the following trades (generally reserved for free blacks in

Cuba): tailor, painter, confectioner, cook. His liberty, so long in coming, was depicted at an earlier date as a melancholy desire in the following lines written to Del Monte in 1834: "When I look over the huge number of accumulated vicissitudes that have upset the most precious days of my youth with terrible blows, I tremble, I tremble not because of the past, but because of what mysteriously remains in the urn of my destiny: a sugar mill, a whipping. That for me has so much importance that I tremble at the mere thought of it."[31]

Depression and disillusionment, born of the frustration of the delay in securing his freedom, undermined his vital energies and contributed to his later silence. In the same moving letter to Del Monte, Manzano touches on questions of envy and mortification of which he was the victim, and writes, "If I had bared my feeling to others as I have to you, perhaps others would not have judged so lightly my love of freedom." Following this he reveals his spiritual exhaustion: "Since on the sea of life, Sir, you've taken command of the rudder of this boat whose destiny was to float aimlessly, in your hands I leave it, and since I am tired of rowing and never reaching port I hope, Sir, you will guide it." The reading of these lines explains why so many tormented pages of the *Autobiography* have been compared to José Martí's *El presidio político en Cuba* (The Political Prison in Cuba),[32] which evokes the nightmares of forced hard labor, punishment, and illness in a Spanish prison on the island of Cuba some three decades later.

To which period of Manzano's life does his *Autobiography* belong? Emilio Roig de Leuchesring, in his introductory remarks to the Franco edition, gives the year 1839,[33] the same date that Franco gives: "Del Monte, his protector and friend, convinced him to write the bitter memoirs of his life as a slave, and the poet wrote his *Autobiography* in 1839 in two parts."[34]

There is no doubt whatsoever that Manzano wrote his *Autobiography* at Del Monte's insistence, for in a letter written to the latter, dated in Havana on 25 June 1835, Manzano writes:

> Your grace, I received your esteemed letter dated the fifteenth of June, and I was surprised that in it your grace says that three or four months ago you asked me for the story of my life. I can only say that I have not

received a request with that amount of notice, *thus on the very same day I received yours of the twenty-second,* I began to turn over in my mind the events of my life, and when I could, I put pen to paper, thinking that a *real*[35] worth of paper would be enough. But I've written somewhat more, and even though I've jumped over periods of four and sometimes five years, I still haven't reached 1820. But I hope to finish soon, *limiting myself only to the most interesting events.* (emphasis added)[36]

From these words we can conclude that Del Monte asked Manzano for the story of his life (but did he instruct Manzano which "interesting events" to stress?) and that the latter began to write it in June of 1835. We might further speculate that he did not finish the second part until 1839, which would justify the date indicated by Leuchesring and Franco. It could not have been later than this date, because when R. R. Madden departed from Cuba in 1839[37] he took with him a portfolio of antislavery literature that Del Monte had put together. Among this material was the *Autobiography,* copied and corrected by Anselmo Suárez y Romero (1818–78).

Social and Historical Contexts

Manzano and Suárez y Romero were members of a group of young writers who gathered around Domingo Del Monte, with whose help several major works were generated that contributed to the development of a genuinely Cuban literary culture. Sugar dominated Cuba's economy in this period, and slavery was considered a necessity for the continued prosperity of the island. However, the most enlightened Cuban intellectuals of the time realized that slavery was a cancer destroying the moral fiber of all sectors of the population and that it was only a matter of time before both moral conscience and economic reality would dictate its abolition. The testimony of Francisco Calcagno, in his novel *Romualdo, uno de tantos* (Romualdo, One among Many), reflects the ideological environment of the 1830s: "We are in the year of 1836. Times are changing: today the slave merchants are beginning to be ashamed of their profession. And it will probably

not be long before we will be ashamed of owning slaves. For now there's no reason to reproach anyone for what we all practice: we have the obligation of enlightening people and breaking the veil of concern in order to prepare the day of justice and honor. There's no crime in being a master; only in abusing that role."[38]

In the face of prevailing social imperfections accepted by the dominant social classes (e.g., Calcagno's approbation of the role of the master vis-à-vis the slave), the Del Monte group's social aspiration was to prepare Cuban society for the future by improving customs and morals.[39] But in view of the fact that most members of the group were allied in some way with the economic interests of the wealthy landowners, particularly of the sugar plantations (without necessarily owning plantations themselves), their strategy was not to move too quickly toward change (i.e., abolition). Hence, they were *not* proponents of abolition, nor did they propose separation from Spain, for that, too, might create unsettling if not disastrous economic consequences for the dominant economic interests on the island. The Del Monte group's position was basically reformist; it hoped that by working within the existing sociopolitical and economic structures it would be able to bring about gradual but significant changes. Its strategy embraced the notion that Spain would offer a solution for the colonial ills—either through representation in the Spanish Cortes or by granting political liberties on the island or both—and that such measures would avoid a war of independence. A Spanish solution, according to Del Monte, would obviate what he feared would be a horrifying uprising of slaves that would deliver the island into the hands of natural, ferocious instincts.[40]

Reforms were certainly in order, for, among other problems, social customs of the time were reputed to be crude and unpolished and the environment stifling, even in the eyes of a foreign observer such as the U.S. writer Richard Henry Dana. Of his short visit to the island Dana left the following notations about Cuba's authoritarian regime:

> Since 1836, Cuba has been deprived of its right to a delegation in the Cortes. Since 1825, vestiges of anything approaching to popular assemblies, juntas,

a jury, independent tribunals, a right of voting, or a right to bear arms, have vanished from the island. The press is under censorship; and so are the theatres and operas. When "I Puritani" is played, the singers are required to substitute Lealtà for Libertà, and one singer was fined and imprisoned for recusancy; and Facciolo, the printer of a secretly circulated newspaper, advocating the cause of Cuban independence, was garroted. The power of banishing, without a charge made, or a trial, or even a record, but on the mere will of the Captain-General, persons whose presence he thinks, or professes to think, prejudicial to the government, whatever their condition, rank, or office, has been frequently exercised, and hangs at all hours over the head of every Cuban.[41]

Del Monte was well aware of these and other short-comings of the colonial government and accordingly felt it was urgent to find viable solutions for the island's social, political, and economic ills. He was a man of unshakable moral convictions— tempered, to be sure, by the limitations any privileged landowner of the period felt whenever the interests of the sacharocracy were threatened. To his initiative we owe Manzano's freedom; and it was he who urged the writing of antislavery works such as Anselmo Suárez y Romero's *Francisco*. As we have already noted, without Del Monte's insistence and stimulus Manzano would never have written his account of the tyrannies of the Cuban slave system.

In spite of the economic interests of his family,[42] Del Monte sincerely defended the notion of providing for a more humane treatment of the slaves. A follower of eighteenth-century ideals of human rights and liberty and a disciple of the French philosopher Victor Cousin, Del Monte considered liberty an inviolate right protected by rational and moral laws of human conduct. José Martí once referred to Del Monte as the most useful Cuban of his time, and indeed he was, not only in the sense Martí suggested but in relation to the life and work of Manzano.

When and under what circumstances did the slave and his mentor meet? We do not know for sure. It is fair, however,

to speculate that Del Monte read Manzano's published verses, or that the members of his literary circle brought them to his attention. Madden, for example, supports the notion that while Manzano was still a slave near Matanzas his poems reached Havana, where they attracted the attention of contemporary literary figures.[43]

The fact that Manzano was a slave intensified interest in his early literary production. According to José Antonio Fernández de Castro, there were other poets of color in this period besides the well-known Plácido (Gabriel de la Concepción Valdés): Ambrosio Echemendia, Agustín Baldomero Rodríguez, Antonio Medina y Céspedes, Juan B. Estrada, Vicente Silveira, and José del Carmen Díaz. But unlike black poets of the twentieth century, Manzano's contemporaries were reticent about alluding to their race and all avoided the mention of slavery.[44] (More than likely, with the exception of José del Carmen Díaz, all of these poets were, like Plácido, free blacks.)[45] It is not surprising that they should have avoided the topic of slavery in their poetry. Slavery, noted Madden, was carefully protected by official censors of all proposed published writing.[46] Even Del Monte was a victim of these censors, who struck eight verses dealing with slavery from his *Romances cubanos* (Cuban Ballads) (1829–33):

> I never could bear hearing,
> without being consumed in ire,
> the barbaric and atrocious sound
> of the whip on a slave's flesh.
>
> And, proud, I much preferred
> to live in poverty, but without stain,
> rather than in infamous opulence,
> at an infamous price bought.

If well-connected Creoles were silenced when they touched on the sensitive issue of slavery, how was it, one might ask, that a slave dared to put pen to paper to describe his tortured existence? The perils of writing an autobiographical account were certainly greater for a slave who was already a public figure, for Manzano, at this point in his career, had already published two

volumes of poetry: *Poesías líricas* (Lyric Poetry) (1821) and *Flores pasajeras* (Ephemeral Flowers) (1830). In addition, his work had appeared in major periodicals such as *La Moda, El Pasatiempo,* and *El Aguinaldo Habanero.* Why, then, did Manzano decide to place in peril his reputation as a rising literary star and run the risk of punishment either by his mistress or at the hands of the official censors?

To begin with, Manzano was confident that the prudent Del Monte would not disseminate the autobiography while the person who gave him such grief in his life as a slave was still alive.[47] But Manzano's real motivation was psychological and emotional in nature: his overriding desire to be released from servitude and enjoy what he himself termed "the natural right that every slave has to his ransom."[48] Manzano never tires of repeating this deep-seated compulsion to Del Monte. In view of the fact that he knew he would be beholden to Del Monte for his freedom, Manzano in reality had no choice but to accede to his benefactor's demand that he produce a history of his life. We can also ask ourselves questions regarding the genesis of this work from the opposite point of view, that is, why would Del Monte, who had the experience of censorship of his antislavery verses and who was aware of the dangers of discussing issues connected with slavery, ask a slave to write the history of his life? And why endanger Manzano's safety and well-being, particularly in the period after 1834 during Captain-General Miguel Tacón's "reign of terror"?

In the face of these various unknowns tied to the history of the peoples without history, there are more questions than answers. However, we do know for a fact that Del Monte intended to publish Manzano's *Autobiography* as well as a number of his poems in Europe rather than on the island.[49] And indeed, it turned out that both the autobiography and some of his poems were translated into English by Madden and published in London. But in 1835, when Del Monte asked Manzano for his memoirs, Madden had not yet arrived in Cuba. Nor had he accepted the appointment to the Mixed Commission,[50] for which reason it is not reasonable to speculate that Del Monte was already thinking of the portfolio of antislavery literature that he would later present to the Irish diplomat.

Whatever the motives or reasons, we are fortunate that Del Monte was successful in persuading Manzano to write this poignant account. Had he not, we would be without a single narrative of slavery in Spanish written by a slave. Its writing was almost as doubtful as the decision to accede to Del Monte's request. The slave began the account but confessed that he almost decided to abandon the project in midstream: "More than four times I decided to leave it unfinished."[51] He also tells us that he would have liked to include details other than his various misfortunes, and he complains about "filling the history of my life [with] the excessive severity with which my former mistress [the Marchioness de Prado Ameno] treated me, forcing me or placing me in the unavoidable situation of resolving to flee in order to save my body from the continuous mortification that I could no longer tolerate." In this same letter, the slave, convinced that he should write the history of his life though still reluctant to do so, warns Del Monte that he must prepare himself to "see a weak creature groveling in the most disconsolate suffering at the hands of various overseers, and without the least consideration, the object of misfortunes."[52]

Clearly Manzano was reluctant to reveal the circumstances of his life. In the first place, he considered himself a person of superior intelligence who merited something better than the condition of a slave. He had been the object of derision on the part of envious, mediocre people because he insisted on his liberty, and one can suppose that he did not wish to suffer further mortifications by laying bare the details of his past life. Besides, it was his fervent desire to make the leap to "white society," and this desire—sometimes conscious, sometimes unconscious—motivated his vacillation in accepting Del Monte's request. Thus, he implored Del Monte to read his autobiography with benevolence: "Remember, your grace, when you read it that *I am a slave and that a slave is a dead soul before his master, and [I hope] I will not lose the esteem I've gained in your eyes*" (emphasis added).[53] He goes on to insist that Del Monte consider him a martyr whose endless whippings "never debased your most affectionate servant."[54]

Added to all of these reasons for his sense of anxiety and distrust with regard to the writing of his autobiography was another that only the fear of displeasing Del Monte could have

overcome. Early in 1835 Manzano married his beloved Delia, "the daughter of a white man, a light-skinned free mulatta, nineteen years of age, beautiful as a gold coin."[55] Her family's opposition to the marriage was inevitable, since Manzano was both darker-skinned and a slave. On several occasions he alluded to her parents' discomfort with the match, speaking of "the conflict my marriage is experiencing"[56] and noting that "all her family is grumbling and making fun of her decision."[57] We can well imagine the unpleasant moments the poet suffered because his liberation was longer in coming than he and Delia's family expected: "The liberty I was promised in this house appears to have disappeared with the wind, like words"; and linking this thought to his wife's chagrin, he adds, "My wife is seven months pregnant and has almost miscarried on three separate occasions because of the displeasures and annoyances occasioned by . . ."[58] And the slave suffers in silence. His wish to conceal his enslavement from public scrutiny, given the racial and social environment of the period, is not unusual; because of his personal and family circumstances he would prefer not to have the story of his life as a slave circulate and further exacerbate his already tenuous relationship with Delia's family. For the latter, fame and distinction as a man of letters clearly compensated to some degree for his darker skin and his enslavement. However, there also was the question of the reaction of his mistress, the marchioness, whose influence could surely cause his imprisonment were she to know of his decision to write about his life as a slave.

Above and beyond all of these personal and circumstantial reasons, it is conceivable that Manzano's reserve with regard to writing his memoirs was generated by apprehensions attributable to his mentor's ideas on slavery. Manzano's insistence on the debased nature of the slave, on the one hand, and his fear of losing Del Monte's esteem, on the other, reflect— even in the dialectic of their construction—Del Monte's ideas expressed forthrightly in "El informe sobre el estado actual de la enseñanza primaria de la Isla de Cuba en 1836, su costo y mejoras de que es susceptible" (Report on the Present State of Elementary Education in Cuba, 1836, Its Cost and Its Possible Reforms):

A person who is born and brought up as a slave, whatever his color or race, must be, because of this state, base, stupid and immoral; and to have these defects is as much part of his basic nature as it is the sun's to shine, and solid bodies' to find the center of their gravity when they are thrown into space. One of the redeeming aspects of human nature, to be sure, is that *there are races, such as the Ethiopian,*[59] *in which one finds generous exceptions to this rule,* but they are not sufficient to change it, for to do so would upset the admirable order that Providence has placed in the governance of the world. (emphasis added)[60]

It is easy to conjecture that Del Monte considered Manzano a generous exception to the immoral state of the slave, a condition that, by the way, in conformity with the more progressive, liberal thinking of the period, he also felt had tainted the masters.

Constructing the Self

Manzano's *Autobiography*, like all personal accounts, is a structured composite of the internal world of the writer and a portion of a reconstructed external universe tied to his personal experience; the two voices are reconstituted so that internal and external history (that of the individual and his collectivity) meld into a single, new construction. In Manzano's text, the slave, portrayed by Manzano, is the victim of the conflict of two visions—that of the slave and that of the master. But in writing of his life, Manzano is careful not to broach the question of slavery's immorality or question the codes of the master discourse. His attention is centered on individual experiences that, taken together, underscore slavery's injustices; as readers, however, we receive and interpret his memoirs as a narration of an abominable system of economic exploitation. The subject moves between happy and somber notes, thus creating the image of a contradictory being, successively docile, rebellious, sad, euphoric, innocent, and mundane.

This ambivalence is characteristic of Manzano's existence, and, in the end, it destroyed his will. Del Monte had

pointed out that the consequences of slavery would touch both masters and slaves, and the most intelligent observer of the period concurred in affirming that slavery was potentially a "mine that would blow all of us up."[61] In his text, Manzano, an agonist of the institution, presents many of its most appalling aspects.

The strategic use of detail in the *Autobiography* is often unexpected and at times curious. Toward the beginning of his account Manzano offers information about the life of his parents, noting their qualities, privileges, and social position, with the purpose, perhaps, of establishing, by reflection or kinship, what he considered his rightful, elevated, or special slave status. However, it is not until the end of the first part that he comments on a detail that is key but which it appears he did not consider of major importance until the critical moment of flight from the marchioness's house. At that moment he describes himself as "a mulatto among blacks," that is, an individual disconnected from his African kin and shut off from the world of the Creole or Spanish whites. Similarly, among the many items concerning his family we find not a single comment about his family name; instead he follows the slave custom of taking his master's surname rather than his father's. These are but two of many illustrations in this text of the silences and omissions attributable to the tortuous dualisms and contradictions created by institutionalized slavery.

Instead of the usual details we might expect to find in an autobiographical history, Manzano begins his narration with an account about his first mistress, Doña Beatriz de Justiz, Marchioness de Santa Ana and wife of Don Juan Manzano, whose custom it was to surround herself with a group of female slaves, all chosen with exquisite care. His mother, he tells us, was one of these "elite" slaves, a servant singled out for training ("criada de razón"). He underscores the theme of special treatment by stating that he too was singled out by his first mistress and kept apart from other slaves, a pattern that, taken as a whole, explains the anguish, trauma, and, later, the breakdown of his will when faced with life's starker realities. He goes on to explain that he was the favored child of the house; his mistress embraced, caressed, spoiled, and protected him. Juan Francisco was for her "the child of her old age." He was not subject to the usual punishments of a child slave, or even the more benign castigations of a white child.

It was only much later in life that he experienced the whippings slaves usually received. Hence his difficulty in subsequent years in dealing with physical punishment that he considered unmerited and cruel.

The Marchioness de Santa Ana evidently spoiled him. But his parents compounded the problem by not correcting him when he misbehaved. On the other hand, as he himself relates, the fault in this matter was also his mistress's; she prohibited his parents from assuming their usual parental functions in guiding and chastising him as a child. In addition, his father, who was of a dry and austere nature, encouraged his "white" illusions by specifically prohibiting him from mingling with other black children ("negritos," Manzano calls them) of the master house, and, similarly, Doña Joaquina Gutiérrez y Zaya, who "would dress me, comb my hair, and take care that I did not mix with the other black children," reinforced his separation from other slaves of his age.

The thematic threads that unify the sometimes confusing chronology of this occasionally chaotic narration are the tribulations of adolescent and young adult life; the struggle to achieve freedom in the face of adverse circumstances; and the determination to learn to read, write, and draw. The latter was a painful process that transformed his life; it provided him with the skills that ultimately made him a famous writer in the tradition of the neoclassic Spanish poet, Juan Bautista de Arriaza y Supervilla (1770–1837), whose verses he admired and imitated.

The chronology of Manzano's work is linked to a construct whose components are more subjective than temporal. Sometimes the young Manzano—following a dualistic narrative pattern—offers abundant details, particularly with regard to those instants of his life that deal with decisive moments of either triumph or depression. At other times, however, there is a sparseness and indefinition that leaves the reader stranded or perplexed: "But let us jump from 1810, 1811, and 1812 to 1835 in the present"; or, in a self-reflexive commentary that lays bare one of his key narrative strategies: "I will limit myself solely to the most essential ones [painful incidents] as fountain or wellspring of a thousand other sorrowful vicissitudes." He remembers his days with the Marchioness de Santa Ana with cheer; later, with equal

joy, he recalls his service in the home of Don Nicolás de Cárdenas y Manzano, with whom he learned to read and write in spite of his benevolent admonition to "abandon that pastime, which did not correspond to my class, and to look for something to sew." This, it should be noted, was said by a man who loved Manzano "not as a slave, but as a son, notwithstanding his young age."

It is in the service of the capricious, domineering, and sadistic Marchioness de Prado Ameno that Manzano's life turns hostile. His mistress is alternatively generous and cruel: she subjects him to whippings, lockups, the stocks, field work; and as a complement to her emotional vacillations, Manzano is alternatively loyal, affectionate, hateful, and resentful. It was in the service of the marchioness that one day he heard the terrifying prediction that he was destined to be "worse than Rousseau and Voltaire," a pronouncement that later failed to worry him when he found out that both were devils and enemies of God. Manzano's religious faith was unshakable; so devoted was he to all the saints that if something terrible befell him he attributed the mishap to his lack of devotion and took it as a sign of divine anger for his less than fervent prayers. His mistress seemed less concerned with religion and was not at all given to charitable deeds. She took special pleasure in torturing her young slave, who was the object of her periodic sadism. For the slightest suspicion of wrongdoing she sent him to the fields, his head shaved, his hands and feet tied, and with instructions to the overseer to punish him by holding back his food, whipping him, placing him in the stocks, and making him work in the sugar fields, a form of labor for which the frail body of the urban slave was unprepared. These periodic punishments and, above all, his mistress's sudden and unjust bouts of anger finally had the effect of creating in him a chronic depression, which he found difficult to overcome. It is in this period of his misery that he began to compose verses, all of them sad, all of them written in the "notebook of his memory," as he puts it, because he did not yet know how to read or write. Through the medium of poetry, the tortured slave found release and solace.

The reading of this poignant text is sufficient to condemn the institution of slavery. The contemporary reader may ask—as perhaps the members of Del Monte's circle did—if it was not the

intention of the slave to demonstrate through the selective details he included in his autobiography that slavery had not vilified him. After all, would this not confirm Del Monte's thesis that there are "generous exceptions," a narrative strategy that would certainly place him in a more positive light and in the process confirm the notion that Del Monte and his followers espoused, namely, that slaves merited more humane treatment.

In spite of what appears to be his innate servility, Manzano, like Esteban Montejo, had no choice but to resolve his untenable situation by taking flight. The instances of rebellion increase as we approach the end of the first part of the *Autobiography*, especially in the light of his mistress's increasing erratic behavior: "As for me, from the moment I lost the rosy illusion to hope, I was no longer a faithful slave." His mistress deceived him, she denied him the freedom bought and paid for by his adoring mother, who could not suffer the anguish and constant mortifications her son received at the hands of the marchioness. In a moment of contrition she promised Juan Francisco that when he came of age and had a trade she would grant him his freedom. But the young slave, desperate for a quick and safe solution, decided to run away.

Manzano in this narration emerges as the incarnation of the slave figure that the novelists of the Del Monte group created, that is, a generous and noble exception to a degraded race, a fundamentally obedient and faithful servant. But besides being submissive, Manzano was fearful. The sudden appearance of the plantation overseer, Don Saturnino, in the marchioness's house and the urging of a free mulatto strengthened his resolve to escape.

In the construction of Manzano's persona it should be noted that there are features different from those of the passive slave in the novels of the period: Manzano was a slave with impressive cultural attainments, and he lead a life of unjustifiable servitude, since the price of his freedom had been fixed and paid for by his mother. These exceptional qualities, coupled with the effects of the treatment he had received from his first mistress as well as from his parents, created illusory expectations that conflicted with reality and contributed to the emotional crisis following his freedom. The genesis and evolution of Manzano's

psychological profile constitutes one of the most remarkable aspects of this *Autobiography*.

A Lost Manuscript

At the end of the first part of his account, Manzano writes, "We shall see what happened to me later in the second part of this story which follows." But the second part disappeared shortly after it was corrected and copied. "The first [part] was turned over to Suárez y Romero, who made a clean copy for Richard R. Madden; the second part was lost by Ramón de Palma (1812–1860) and was never found."[62] Madden lost no time in translating (albeit inaccurately) sections of the first part. In 1840 his version appeared in London together with other antislavery pieces in a volume entitled *Poems by a Slave in the Island of Cuba, recently liberated; translated from the Spanish by R. R. Madden, M.D., with a History of the early life of the Negro Poet written by Himself; to which are prefixed two pieces descriptive of Cuban Slavery and the Slave Traffic.*

In his introduction, Madden is more specific with regard to the second part, which, in his opinion "fell into the hands of persons connected with his former master, and I fear it is not likely to be restored to the person to whom I am indebted for the first portion of this manuscript."[63] (If Madden's remarks are accurate, they constitute a sign of slavery's subjugation of the subject: note that his suggestion is that the manuscript be returned *not* to the author, but to his mentor.)

The original from which Suárez y Romero copied, according to Franco, is in the José Martí National Library of Cuba.[64] From this copy Franco produced his edition of the Manzano text in Spanish—just about a hundred years after its appearance in English—incorporating in it all its errors, including its "abominable orthography."[65] The original lacks the most elementary notions of punctuation and syntax, for which reason we took the liberty in 1975 of modernizing the text. Though there are some who would object to modifications because they distort the original, whose defects are the mark of slavery, the modern reader of either Spanish or English would find the original text or its direct translation a chore to read.[66] In preparing our Spanish

version we followed Franco's lead: in the prologue to his edition he corrects and modernizes sections of the Manzano text.[67] In dividing paragraphs, separating sentences, and regularizing punctuation and orthography we were and are aware of the fact that, as Cintio Vitier has noted, "it is not the same to read his emotional *Autobiography* correctly written as it is with its errors. These shortcomings inspire respect, because they are not, strictly speaking, shortcomings: they are like scars on his body."[68] The second part of the text, whose disappearance remains an enigma, would surely have thrown a great deal of light on these scars and might well have given us information about Manzano's silence following his liberation.

The fact is, Manzano did not abandon writing completely after attaining his freedom. His contributions to *El Aguinaldo Habanero* (1837) and *El Album* (1838) belong to his postslave period, as does his drama *Zafira* (1842). But his production as a writer suffered an evident decline. Until new evidence comes to light, we are disposed to reaffirm our view that once the tension connected to his central desire in life—his freedom—disappeared and he was faced with the limitations colonial Cuban society and culture placed on a person of color, he lost his sense of purpose in life and succumbed to a protracted despondency.

One might ask, in this regard, what became of the proposed project he suggested in 1835, of reserving the most interesting events of his life and writing a Cuban novel based on them—that is, once his life was stable, he was free, and his finances were secure.[69] Did earning his living take up all his time? As a slave he had less time and none of the freedom he later enjoyed, and yet he found time to produce both prose and poetry. We return thus to our theory that his life following liberation was one of personal and social frustration and disappointment. The final blow must have been Plácido's false accusation, in 1844, that Manzano—together with Del Monte—was involved in the Escalera Conspiracy of blacks and mulattos against the Spanish colonial system in Cuba.

A letter written to Rosa Aldama, Del Monte's wife, from the jail where he languished following the accusation, reveals not only his innocence but the nature of his moral fiber, his sensitivity, and the perennial difficulties of navigating between

the world of white hegemony and that of marginalized blacks, without ever belonging to one or the other.

Manzano gained his second freedom—this time from his unjust imprisonment by the colonial authorities—in 1845. But his disillusionment was such, his spirit so broken by the experience, that in the nine years left in his life he never produced any literature. But what he did leave us, especially his autobiography, constitutes, as Madden noted, "the most perfect picture of Cuban slavery that has ever been given to the world."[70]

Chronology

1797? Juan Francisco Manzano is born in the Marchioness Justiz de Santa Ana's house, where his mother is a slave. He is given the surname of the marchioness's husband.

1809 The Marchioness de Santa Ana dies, and Manzano becomes the property, first of his godmother, Doña Trinidad de Zayas, and then of the Marchioness de Prado Ameno.

1814?–1817? Escapes to Havana.

1818 Enters the service of Don Nicolás de Cárdenas y Manzano, second son of the Marchioness de Prado Ameno.

1821 Enters the service of Don Tello Mantilla in Havana.

1821 Publishes *Cantos a Lesbia* (Songs to Lesbia).

1830 Introduced to Domingo Del Monte, who is later instrumental in obtaining his freedom.

1831 Del Monte publishes Manzano's poem "Al nacimiento de la Infanta María Isabel de Luisa de Borbón" (On the birth of the Infanta María Isabel de Luisa de Borbón) in *La Moda*.

1830–1838 Publishes poetry in *Diario de la Habana*.

1834 Publishes his "Romances cubanos" (Cuban Ballads) in *El Pasatiempo* (Matanzas).

1835 2 March: Marries María del Rosario Díaz ("Delia"). This is Manzano's second marriage. He was widowed in his first (date unknown), with Marcelina Campos.

1836 Manzano gains his freedom.

1837–1838 Publishes poems in *El Aguinaldo Habanero* and *El Album*.

1839 Completes the two parts of the *Autobiography* (the second part was lost).

1840 R. R. Madden publishes part of the *Autobiography* (translated into English) and some of Manzano's poems (in English) under the title *Poems by a Slave in the Island of Cuba, recently liberated.* V. Schoelcher translates part of the *Autobiography* into French.

1853 Death of Manzano in Havana.

1937 First Spanish edition of the *Autobiography*, based on a manuscript in the National Archives in Havana.

Notes

1. Letter to Domingo Del Monte, 25 June 1835, in *Autobiografía, cartas y versos de Juan Francisco Manzano* (Autobiography, Letters, and Poetry by Juan Francisco Manzano), ed. José L. Franco (Havana: Muncipio de la Habana, 1937), 84.

2. In fact, it was never published in the nineteenth century in Cuba. Its first publication in book form was in 1937 (see note 1).

3. Alexander Humboldt, *Ensayo político sobre la isla de Cuba* (Political Essay about the Island of Cuba) (Havana: Lex, 1960), 148. All translations, unless otherwise indicated, are mine.

4. Manzano refers to his ransom (*rescate*), that is, the price of his manumission, in a letter to Del Monte, 16 October 1835 (Franco, 86).

5. Fernando Ortiz, *Los negros esclavos* (The African Slaves) (Havana: Revista Bimestre Cubana, 1916), 321.

6. For a detailed introductory account of Cuba's economic history during this period, see Hugh Thomas, *Cuba: The Pursuit of Freedom* (New York: Harper and Row, 1971).

7. Ibid., 142.

8. For a comprehensive bibliography see Franklin W. Knight, *Slave Society in Cuba during the Nineteenth Century* (Madison: University of Wisconsin Press, 1970), 204–20. A more recent, excellent source is Manuel Moreno Fraginal's *El ingenio* (The Sugar-Mill) (Havana: Editorial de Ciencias Sociales, 1978), 3:167–267.

9. On the subject of maroons, that is, runaway slaves, see *Diario del rancheador* (The Diary of a Slave Hunter), published by Roberto Friol in *Revista de la Biblioteca Nacional José Martí* 15 (January–April, 1973): 47–148.

10. Pedro Deschamps Chapeaux, *El negro en la economía habanera del siglo XIX* (The Black in the Havana Economy of the Nineteenth Century) (Havana: UNEAC, 1971), 11.

11. In his reference works on slavery, Fernando Ortiz uses novels and short narratives to illustrate his points. The veracity of

fiction, however, can easily be criticized. See, for example, Barras y Prado (note 12).

12. Antonio de las Barras y Prado, *La Habana a mediados del siglo XIX: Memorias* (Havana in the Mid-Nineteenth Century: Memoirs) (Madrid: Imprenta de la Ciudad Lineal, 1925), 108.

13. José Antonio Portuondo, *Crítica de la época y otros ensayos* (Criticism of the Period and Other Essays) (Santa Clara: Universidad Central de las Villas, 1965), 26.

14. Angel Luis Fernández Guerra, "Cimarrón y Rachel, un 'continuum'" (Maroon and Rachel, a Continuum), *Unión* 9 (December 1970): 166.

15. Miguel Barnet, *Biografía de un cimarrón* (Autobiography of a Runaway Slave) (Mexico: Siglo XXI, 1968), 42.

16. Ibid., 37.

17. Ibid., 198.

18. Ibid., 13.

19. R. R. Madden, *Poems by a Slave in the Island of Cuba, recently liberated; translated from the Spanish, by R. R. Madden, M.D., with the History of the Early Life of the Negro Poet, written by Himself; to which are prefixed two pieces descriptive of Cuban Slavery and the Slave-Traffic* (London: Thomas Ward and Co., 1840), ii.

20. Barnet, 149.

21. Verena Martínez Alier, "El honor de la mujer en Cuba en el siglo XIX" (Women's Honor in Nineteenth-Century Cuba), *Revista de la Biblioteca Nacional José Martí* 13 (May–August 1971): 48–49.

22. Cintio Vitier, "Dos poetas cubanos, Plácido y Manzano" (Two Cuban Poets, Plácido and Manzano), *Bohemia*, 14 December 1973, 21.

23. Franco, 20.

24. Facts cited in Calcagno's introduction to Manzano's drama *Zafira* (Havana: Consejo Nacional de Cultura, 1962), 5.

25. Francisco Calcagno, *Diccionario biográfico cubano* (New York: Ponce de León, 1878).

26. Madden, iv.

27. We cite from the translation provided by Madden in his 1840 edition of Manzano (101).

28. If he read these verses in 1836, then he must have been born in 1806.
29. Franco, 27.
30. Vitier, 19.
31. Franco, 80.
32. Vitier, 20.
33. n.pag.
34. Franco, 28.
35. A monetary unit of Spanish origin.
36. Franco, 83.
37. See David R. Murray, "Richard Robert Madden: His Career as a Slavery Abolitionist," *Studies* 61 (Spring 1972): 41–53.
38. From a fragment of Calcagno's novel published in *Islas* 44 (January–February 1973): 107–8.
39. See, for example, José Z. González del Valle, *La vida literaria en Cuba (1836–1840)* (Literary Life in Cuba [1836–1840]) (Havana: Publicaciones de la Secretaría de Educación Pública, 1938), 5–6.
40. Domingo Del Monte, *Escritos*. 2 vols. (Havana: Cultural, 1929), 1:86.
41. Richard Henry Dana, *To Cuba and Back: A Vacation Voyage* (Boston: Houghton, Mifflin, 1859), 233.
42. He was the son-in-law of Domingo Aldama, one of the wealthiest sugar plantation owners on the island.
43. Madden, i.
44. José Antonio Fernández de Castro, *El tema negro en las letras de Cuba (1608–1935)* (The Theme of the Black in Cuban Literature [1608–1935]) (Havana: Ediciones Mirador, 1943).
45. G. R. Coulthard notes that Rodríguez, Medina, and Díaz were born slaves and that the freedom of José del Carmen Díaz was bought with the proceeds of the 1879 *Poetas de color* (Poets of Color), by Francisco Calcagno. See Coulthard, *Raza y color en la literatura antillana* (Race and Color in Antillean Literature) (Seville: Escuela de Estudios Hispano-Americanos, 1958), 26–27.
46. Madden, i.
47. Letter to Del Monte, 25 June 1835, in Franco, 84.
48. Ibid.
49. In the 11 December 1834 letter to Del Monte, Manzano

writes, "Your grace, I cannot describe the enormous surprise I felt when I learned from you your plans for my poetry. When I think of it circulating in distant climes in order to see the light of day in the emporium of European learning . . ." (in Franco, 80).

50. Madden was appointed in the spring of 1836, and the Spanish government was advised in May of the same year (Murray, 48).

51. Letter to Del Monte, 25 June 1835, in Franco, 83.

52. Ibid., 84.

53. Ibid.

54. Ibid.

55. Letter to Del Monte, 11 December 1834, in Franco, 84.

56. Ibid.

57. Letter to Del Monte, 25 February 1835, in Franco, 83.

58. Letter to Del Monte, 29 September 1835, in Franco, 85.

59. The Spanish *etíope* (Ethiopian) was used to refer to all blacks.

60. Del Monte, *Escritos*, 2:43.

61. Ibid., 1:44.

62. Franco, 28.

63. Madden, iv.

64. Franco, 29.

65. Ibid., 26.

66. Sylvia Molloy, in *At Face Value: Autobiographical Writing in Spanish America* (Cambridge: Cambridge University Press, 1991), contends that the "underwritten" quality of the original manuscript reflects the absence of models, or, as she puts it, of a "*master* image" (53). The disparity between the more "polished" style of the poetry and the somewhat more "primitive" quality of the *Autobiography* has always been a mystery, and will in all likelihood continue to be one. Did Del Monte or his disciples correct the poems more than the autobiography? In the Vidal Morales manuscript, prepared by Suárez y Romero, much more is corrected and changed (compared with the original notebook manuscript reproduced by Franco) than Suárez y Romero is willing to confess in a 1875 letter: "When I corrected the original I did little more than touch the orthography, leaving the original words and constructions used by the author" (ms. in the José

Martí National Library). But Molloy's contention that there were no models is not accurate; there were prose models written by members of the Del Monte group and also other texts by writers of color in colonial Cuba.

67. See, for example, Franco, 23.
68. Vitier, 20.
69. Letter to Del Monte, 29 September 1835, in Franco, 85.
70. Madden, iv.

Suggested Readings on Juan Francisco Manzano

Del Monte, Domingo. "Dos poetas negros. Plácido y Manzano." (Two Black Poets. Plácido and Manzano.) *Escritos.* (Selected Works.) Havana: Cultural, 1929. 2 149–150.

Friol, Roberto. *Suite para Juan Francisco Manzano.* (Suite for Juan Francisco Manzano.) Havana: Editorial Arte y Literatura, 1977. (Contains vital documentation about Manzano's biography and works.)

Luis, William. "Textual Multiplications: Juan Francisco Manzano's *Autobiografía* and Cirilo Villaverde's *Cecilia Valdés.*" In *Literary Bondage: Slavery in Cuban Narrative,* 27–81. Austin: University of Texas Press, 1990.

Manzano, Juan Francisco. *Obras.* Ed. José Luciano Franco. Havana: Instituto del Libro, 1972.

Molloy, Sylvia. "From Serf to Self: The Autobiography of Juan Francisco Manzano." In *At Face Value; Autobiographical Writing in Spanish America,* 36–54. Cambridge: Cambridge University Press, 1991.

Schulman, Ivan A. "Juan Francisco Manzano or the Resurrection of a Dead Soul." *Review* (Center for Inter-American Relations) 31 (January–April 1983): 60–62.

———. "Invención y disfraz: El discurso cubano de la *Autobiografía* de Juan Francisco Manzano." (Invention and Mask: The Discourse of the Autobiography of Juan Francisco Manzano.) In *Discursos sobre la invención de América* (Discourses on the Invention of America), edited by Iris M. Zavala, 167–81. Amsterdam: Rodopi, 1992.

POEMS

by

A SLAVE IN THE ISLAND OF CUBA,

RECENTLY LIBERATED;

TRANSLATED FROM THE SPANISH,

by

R. R. MADDEN, M.D.

WITH THE HISTORY OF THE

EARLY LIFE OF THE NEGRO POET,

WRITTEN BY HIMSELF

TO WHICH ARE PREFIXED

TWO PIECES DESCRIPTIVE OF

CUBAN SLAVERY AND THE SLAVE-TRAFFIC,

By R. R. M.

LONDON:
THOMAS WARD AND CO.,
27, PATERNOSTER ROW;
AND MAY BE HAD AT THE OFFICE OF THE BRITISH AND FOREIGN
ANTI-SLAVERY SOCIETY, 27, NEW BROAD STREET.
1840.

Title page of the volume in which Manzano's autobiography appeared (in part) for the first time in printed form in any language.

Female slave with child in sugar cane field. (Illustration from the R. R. Madden edition of the autobiography, 1840.)

Casa de paila. *Refining sugar on the plantation. (Anonymous German lithograph, c. 1850.)*

Cutting cane. (Wood engraving by Jules-Marie-René Ladmiral, c. 1860.)

The Autobiography
of a Slave

Autobiografía
de un esclavo

Autobiografía de
— un esclavo

LA SEÑORA DOÑA BEATRIZ DE JUSTIZ, Marquesa
Justiz de Santa Ana, esposa del señor don Juan Manzano,
cada vez que iba a su famosa hacienda el Molino gustaba de
tomar las más bonitas criollas[1] entre diez y once años. Las traía
consigo, dándoles una educación conforme a su clase y condición.
Así estaba siempre su casa llena de criadas instruidas en todo lo
necesario para su servicio y de este modo no se hacía notar la
falta de las tres o cuatro que no estuviesen aptas para el trabajo
por sus años, dolencias o libertad. Entre las escogidas fue una
María del Pilar Manzano, mi madre, que de la servidumbre de
mano de la señora Marquesa Justiz en su mayor edad, era una de
las criadas de distinción, de estimación, o de *razón*,[2] como quiera
que se le llame.

Tenía también aquella señora por costumbre, después del
esmero con que criaba a estas sus sirvientas, darles la libertad en
donación y de equiparlas del todo como si fuesen hijas propias
el día que se querían casar con algún artesano libre. No por eso
perdían todo el favor y protección de la casa, haciéndose éstos
extensivos hasta sus hijos y esposo, casos de los cuales hay muchos
ejemplos que citar.

---

1. Término usado en la literatura de este período para designar al negro de ascendencia
   africana nacido en la isla.
2. En su manuscrito, Manzano subraya esta palabra, señalando de este modo, desde
   un principio, que nació de una madre esclava de facultades especiales: instrucción,
   entrenamiento. Estas facultades, no asociadas normalmente con los esclavos, ni con
   la educación que éstos recibían, moldean la vida del niño Juan Francisco, creando en
   su alma la noción ilusoria de poder superar su condición de esclavo por medio de sus
   aptitudes intelectuales o el uso del raciocinio.

The Autobiography of a Slave

W HENEVER DOÑA BEATRIZ DE JUSTIZ, the Marchioness Justiz de Santa Ana, wife of Don Juan Manzano, went to El Molino, her famous plantation, she liked to take with her the most beautiful ten- and eleven-year-old Creole[1] girls. She took them along, providing them with an appropriate upbringing for their class and station in society. Her house, therefore, was always full of maids instructed to minister to her every need, so that one did not notice the absence of the three or four who were ill suited for work because of age, ailments, or freedom granted. Among the chosen few, was one María del Pilar Manzano, my mother, who, as handservant in the marchioness's later years, was one of the maids of distinction, esteemed, or singled out for training,[2] however one prefers to put it.

After the care she had taken in raising her servants, the mistress was accustomed to awarding them freedom, providing for them as if they were her own daughters when they decided to marry some freed artisan. In spite of that, they did not forfeit her favor and protection, which she even extended to their children and husbands, and about which there are many noteworthy examples.

---

1. Term used in the literature of the period to refer to the slave of African descent born on the island.
2. In his manuscript Manzano underlines this term, showing in this way, from the beginning, that he was born of a slave mother who possessed special qualities due in part to her training and education. These qualities, not normally associated with slaves or the education they received, molded the life of the young Juan Francisco, creating in his soul the illusory notion of being able to overcome his condition as a slave through his intellectual aptitudes or the use of reason.

De este modo sucedía sin embargo, que los hijos de tales matrimonios no nacían en la casa, y siguiendo este orden y por diversos accidentes, se fue menoscabando el gran número de aquella florida servidumbre. Así vino a ser María del Pilar el todo al servicio de mano de la señora Marquesa. En este estado tuvo aquélla la suerte de ver casar a la señora Condesa de Buenavista y a la señora Marquesa de Prado Ameno, y por casualidad vino a criar al señor don Manuel de Cárdenas y Manzano. Pero no lo crió al pecho, pues habiendo enfermado su criandera,[3] la parda libre Catalina Monzón, le tocó a María del Pilar seguir la cría con todas las dificultades que se infieren en criar a un niño que deja un pecho y no quiere tomar otro.

Iba venciendo todos los obstáculos de la cría del señor don Manuel cuando nació el señor don Nicolás, su hermano, y cuando se verificó el matrimonio de Toribio de Castro con María del Pilar, a quienes debo el ser, saliendo a luz el año de. . . .[4]

Como ya he dicho, no había nacido en la casa ninguno, y mi ama, la señora Marquesa de Justiz, ya señora de edad, me tomó como un género de entretenimiento. Dicen que más estaba yo en sus brazos que en los de mi madre, que, con todos los títulos de una criada de mano y medio criandera, había casado con el primer criado de la casa y dado a su señora un criollo que ella llamaba el niño de su vejez. Aún viven testigos de esta verdad. Crecí al lado de mi señora sin separarme de ella más que para dormir, pues ni al campo viajaba sin llevarme en la volante. Con diferencia de horas para unos, de días para otros, nací contemporáneo del señor don Miguel de Cárdenas y Manzano y del señor don Manuel O'Reilly, hoy Conde de Buenavista y Marqués Justiz de Santa Ana.

Ambas familias vivían en la grandísima y hermosísima casa contigua a La Machina.[5] La casa estaba dividida sólo por

---

3. Nodriza. Pichardo observa: "Así se denomina generalmente; pero no es la expresión más culta. . . ." (Esteban Rodríguez Herrera, ed., *Pichardo novísimo, o diccionario provincial casi razonado de vozes y frases cubanas* [La Habana: Editorial Selecta, 1955]) (de aquí en adelante, citamos el título abreviado: Pichardo novísimo).
4. Es interesante observar que Manzano no recuerda la fecha de su nacimiento, sobre todo en vista de que recuerda otras fechas y los detalles de muchísimos percances de su vida.
5. Probablemente un lugar cerca del puerto de Matanzas donde estaba instalada una grúa del puerto. En su estudio preliminar "Juan Francisco Manzano, el poeta esclavo y su tiempo," José Luciano Franco no ofrece más detalle que "la mansión señorial, situada

So it was, however, that the offspring of such marriages were not born in the marchioness's house, and as a result of this and other mishaps the considerable number of select servants began to dwindle. It was thus that María del Pilar came to be the marchioness's only handmaid. In that position she had the good fortune to witness the marriages of the Countess of Buenavista and the Marchioness de Prado Ameno and, by chance, raised Don Manuel de Cárdenas y Manzano. However, she did not nurse him, but rather took over when his wet nurse, the freed mulatta Carolina Monzón, became ill, leaving her with all the difficulties involved in nursing a baby who, taken from one breast, refuses to suckle from another.

She was just about overcoming all the obstacles of rearing Don Manuel when his brother, Don Nicolás, was born, and when the marriage of those to whom I owe my existence, Toribio de Castro and María del Pilar, came about, as I was born in the year . . . [3]

As I have already stated, no child had been born in the house, and my mistress, the Marchioness de Justiz, by then an elderly lady, adopted me as a form of entertainment. They say she held me in her arms more than my mother, who, with all her titles from handmaid to half-time nurse, had married the head houseservant and provided her mistress with a Creole, which she called the child of her old age. There are still some living witnesses to this fact. I grew up alongside my mistress without leaving her side except to sleep, for she never even traveled to the countryside without taking me along in the coach. Within a difference of hours according to some, days according to others, I was born a contemporary of Don Miguel de Cárdenas and Don Manuel O'Reilly, today the Count of Buenavista and the Marquis Justiz de Santa Ana.

Both families lived in the enormous and very beautiful house next to La Machina.[4] The house was partitioned by only

---

3. It is interesting to note that Manzano does not remember his date of birth, especially in view of the fact that he does remember other dates and the details of many mishaps in his life.
4. Probably a place near Matanzas harbor where there was a crane. In his preliminary study, "Juan Francisco Manzano, el poeta esclavo y su tiempo" (Juan Francisco Manzano, the Slave-Poet and His Times) (*Juan Francisco Manzano, Cartas y versos de Juan Francisco*

algunas puertas que separaban los departamentos, pues eran tres grandes casas reunidas en una. Así sería ocioso pintar cuál andaría yo entre la tropa de nietos de mi señora. Me la pasaba traveseando, mejor mirado de lo que merecía por los favores que me dispensaba mi señora, a quien yo también llamaba "mama mía."

Cumplía yo ya seis años cuando, por ser demasiado vivo, más que todos, se me envió a la escuela en casa de mi madrina de bautismo, Trinidad de Zayas. Se me traía a las doce del día y por la tarde para que mi señora me viera, la cual se guardaba de salir hasta que yo viniese. De no ser así echaba yo la casa abajo, llorando y gritando, y era preciso en este caso apelar a la soba, a lo que nadie se atrevía. Todos se guardaban de dármela, pues ni mis padres se hallaban autorizados para ello, y yo que lo sabía, si tal cosa me hacían, los acusaba. Ocurrió una vez que, estando yo muy majadero, me sacudió mi padre, pero recio. Lo supo mi señora y fue lo bastante para que no lo quisiera ver en muchos días, hasta que, a instancias de su confesor, el padre Moya, religioso de San Francisco, le devolvió su gracia. Esto después de enseñarle a aquél los derechos de padre que conmigo le correspondían como tal, y los que le correspondían a ella como ama, ocupando el lugar de madre.

A la edad de diez años daba yo de memoria los más largos sermones de Fray Luis de Granada, y el numeroso concurso que visitaba la casa en que nací me oía los domingos cuando venía de aprender a oír la Santa Misa con mi madrina. En la casa había misa, pero no se me permitía oírla allí, por el jugueteo y distracción con los otros muchachos.

Tenía ya diez años cuando, instruído en todo cuanto podía instruirme una mujer en asuntos de religión, daba todo el catecismo de memoria, así como casi todos los sermones de Fray Luis de Granada. Sabía además muchas relaciones, loas[6] y entremeses, teoría regular y la colocación de las piezas. Me

---

cerca de la Machina" (*Juan Francisco Manzano, cartas y versos de Juan Francisco Manzano* [La Habana: Municipio de la Habana, 1937], p. 20).

6. Piezas cortas que se representaban antes de la principal o solas.

a few doors that separated the apartments, for they were three large houses joined together into one. It would be pointless, therefore, to describe which one I roamed around in, along with my mistress's crew of grandchildren. I spent my time getting into all kinds of mischief, but was seen in a better light than I deserved because of all the favors bestowed on me by my mistress, whom I also called "my mama."

When I was almost six, and more clever than the others, I was sent to school at the home of my baptismal godmother, Trinidad de Zayas. I was usually brought home at midday and in the evening so that the marchioness might see me, for she refrained from going out before I arrived. If she ever did leave, I raised such a fuss, crying and screaming, that I should have received a beating, but nobody dared do that. Everyone avoided it, for not even my parents were authorized to do so, and I, who knew it, tattled on whomever did such a thing to me. On one occasion my father shook me harshly for being quite unruly. My mistress found out, and that was enough for her to refuse to see my father for several days until she restored him to her good graces at the behest of her confessor, Father Moya, of the Order of San Francisco. She did so only after making clear to him which parental rights were his as a father and which hers as a slaveholder who assumed the role of a mother.

At the age of ten I could recite from memory Fray Luis of Granada's longest sermons, and the stream of visitors to the house where I was born used to listen to me on Sundays when I would come home from learning to listen to sacred mass with my godmother. Mass was heard in the house, but I was not permitted to attend because I would play with and distract the other children.

When I was already ten years old and knowledgeable in all that a woman could teach me about religion, I would recite not only the entire catechism by heart but also almost all of Fray Luis of Granada's sermons. I also knew many lengthy passages, short plays[5] and interludes, dramatic theory, and stage sets. They

---

Manzano [Havana: Municipio de la Habana, 1937], p.20), José Luciano Franco offers only this detail: "the grand mansion located near La Machina."
5. Brief plays that introduced the main play or were performed alone.

llevaron a la ópera francesa y vine remedando a algunos, por lo cual, aunque siempre era más por los sermones, mis padres recibían de mí la porción de galas que recogía en la sala.

Pasando por alto otros pormenores ocurridos durante los días que debía recibir el bautismo, me ceñiré únicamente a lo agradable, pues ahora voy corriendo por un jardín de bellísimas flores, *una serie de felicidades*.[7] Me llevaron a la iglesia envuelto en el faldellín con que se bautizó la señora doña Beatriz de Cárdenas y Manzano y la ceremonia se celebró con arpa, que la tocaba mi padre, y con música de clarinete y flauta. Quiso mi señora marcar este día con una de sus rasgos de generosidad, y coartó[8] a mis padres dejándolos en trescientos pesos por cada uno. Yo debí ser algo más feliz; pero pase.

Tenía yo siete u ocho años, cuando me preguntaban qué oficio tenía y no había uno que yo dijera que ignoraba. En esto parece que leía yo los días que en el porvenir me esperaban.

En la carrera de mi vida llegaba ya el tiempo en que mi ama fuera desprendiéndose de mí para ponerme oficio, como en efecto se verificó. Teniendo yo como diez años se me puso a pupilo con mis padrinos, llevando ya las primeras lecciones de sastre con mi padre.

Entonces viajaba con frecuencia la señora Marquesa Jus-tiz a su hacienda el Molino. Mi madre se declaraba en extremo fecunda, pues ya tenía yo un hermano que me seguía y una hermana que murió del mal llamado Blasa[9] y quien no sé por qué especie de gracia nació libre. (Mi padre se lamentaba de que las cosas hubieran ocurrido así; él estaba contento con sus dos hijos varones que estaban vivos, y total que los otros dos vientres se habían malogrado.) Mas aquella bondadosísima señora, fuente inagotable de gracias, le volvió a renovar un documento en que le

7. El énfasis es de Manzano, pues parecía sentir la necesidad de explicar la imagen anterior "jardín de bellísimas flores."
8. *Coartar*: "Fijar el precio del esclavo invariablemente para no poder exigir más por su venta o manumisión . . ." (*Pichardo novísimo*).
9. No hemos podido identificar esta enfermedad. En el capítulo XV del libro de Fernando Ortiz, "Las enfermedades del esclavo rural," *Los negros esclavos*, no hay mención de ella.

took me to see French operas, and I was good at imitating some of them, for which my parents used to receive the allotment of gifts from me that I would collect in the parlor, although it was always more from the sermons.

Passing over some other details that occurred during the days in which I was to be baptized, I will concentrate only on the pleasant ones, as I am now wandering through a garden of very beautiful flowers, *a series of joys.*[6] They took me to the church in the same baptismal gown used for Doña Beatriz de Cárdenas y Manzano, and the ceremony was performed with a harp played by my father and with clarinet and flute music. My mistress wanted to celebrate that day with one of her generous gestures and officially established my parents' manumission price[7] at three hundred pesos each. I should have been a bit happier; but let's go on.

I was seven or eight years old when they used to ask me what my trade was, and there wasn't a single one I didn't know. On this subject it seems I was foreseeing the days that awaited me in the future.

In the course of my life, the time was coming for my owner to disengage herself from me by finding me a trade, and so, in fact, she did. At about ten years of age, I was apprenticed to my godparents as a pupil, after having my first lessons as a tailor with my father.

In those days the Marchioness de Justiz traveled frequently to her plantation, El Molino. My mother was proving to be very prolific, for after me she had my brother and a sister, who died from the disease called *blasa*[8] and who, only the Lord knows why, was born free. (My father lamented that things had turned out that way; he was satisfied with his two surviving sons, especially since the other two pregnancies were fruitless.) But

---

6. The emphasis is Manzano's. It seems he felt it necessary to explain the previous image, "garden of very beautiful flowers."
7. The slave price is set invariably in order to avoid exacting more for the sale or freedom of the slave (Esteban Rodríguez Herrera, ed., *Pichardo novísimo, o diccionario provincial casi razonado de vozes y frases cubanas* [Havana: Editorial Selecta, 1955]) (hereafter cited as *Pichardo novísimo*).
8. We have been unable to identify this disease. In chapter 15 of Fernando Ortiz's *Los negros esclavos* (The African Slaves) (Havana: Revista Bimestre Cubana, 1916), entitled "The Illnesses of the Rural Slave," it receives no mention.

ofrecí a la libertad del vientre, naciese lo que naciese. Y nacieron mellizos, varón y hembra. Hubo en esto unas diferencias, mas lo terminante del documento hizo que un tribunal diese la libertad a los dos, porque ambos formaron un vientre. La hembra vive aún. Con este motivo mis padres se quedaron en el Molino al cuidado de la casa.

En el período de estos acontecimientos la señora Marquesa Justiz murió en la misma hacienda. Todos sus hijos la asistieron hasta el último momento. Yo me hallaba a la sazón a pupilo en La Habana, pero se le envió una volante a la señora doña Joaquina Gutiérrez y Zayas, la que se presentó en casa de mi madrina y me pidió de parte de mi señora. Al momento se puso en camino conmigo para Matanzas, donde llegamos al segundo día como a la una de la tarde.

Esta época, por lo remota, no está bien fija en mi memoria. Sólo me acuerdo de que mi madre, doña Joaquina, el padre y yo estuvimos en fila en su cuarto. Ella me tenía puesta la mano sobre un hombro. Mi madre y doña Joaquina lloraban. De lo que hablaban, no sé. Salimos de allí y yo me fui a jugar. Sólo me acuerdo de que a la mañana siguiente la vi tendida en una gran cama, que grité y que me llevaron al fondo de la casa, donde estaban las demás criadas enlutadas. En la noche toda la negrada de la hacienda sollozando rezó el rosario. Yo lloraba a mares y me separaron, entregándome a mi padre.

Pasados algunos días o algún tiempo, partimos para La Habana. La misma señora doña Joaquina me condujo a la casa de mi madrina, donde luego supe me había dejado mi señora.

Pasaron algunos años sin que yo viese a mis padres. Creo no equivocarme en decir que habría cinco años, pues me acuerdo de que había vivido mucho tiempo con mi madrina en la calle nueva del Cristo, y que ya cosía e iba a los ejercicios de juego con mi padrino, que era sargento primero de su batallón, Javier Calvo. Luego nos mudamos a la calle del Inquisidor, en el solar del señor Conde de O'Reilly, y vi el bautismo famoso del señor don Pedro O'Reilly a quien vi vestir mamelucos[10] y andar solo

---

10. Especie de *overol*, "vestido enterizo que hacía de camisa y calzones anchos para los niños" (*Pichardo novísimo*).

that most benevolent lady, the source of endless generosities, again renewed a document in which she granted an unborn child freedom, be it boy or girl. And twins were born, male and female. Because of this, there were some legal contradictions, but the decisiveness of the document forced the courts to grant freedom to both of them because they were born at the same time. The girl is still alive. Owing to that, my parents stayed at El Molino in charge of the house.

At about the same time as these events, the Marchioness de Justiz died on the same plantation. All her children were with her until the last moment. At the time I was a pupil in Havana, but a message was sent to Doña Joaquina Gutiérrez y Zayas, who called at my godmother's house and asked for me on behalf of my mistress. She departed with me immediately for Matanzas, where we arrived the next day at about one in the afternoon.

Because it is so distant, this period of time is not very clear in my memory. I only remember that my mother, Doña Joaquina, the priest, and I lined up in my mistress's room. My mother had her hand on my shoulder. She and Doña Joaquina were crying. I do not know what they were talking about. We left the room, and I went out to play. All I remember is that I saw my mistress the next morning laid out on a huge bed, that I screamed, and that they took me to the back of the house, where the other servants were in mourning. That night all the slaves on the plantation wept and recited the rosary. I cried buckets and they took me aside, handing me over to my father.

After a few days or so we left for Havana. Doña Joaquina herself drove me to my godmother's house, an arrangement I later found out had been decreed by my mistress.

A few years went by in which I did not see my parents. I think I am right to say it was probably five years, because I remember having lived with my godmother a long time on new Christ Street and that I was already sewing and attending military drills with my godfather, Javier Calvo, a first sergeant in his battalion. Later we moved to the ancestral home of Count O'Reilly on Inquisitor Street, and I saw the famous baptism of Don Pedro O'Reilly, whom I knew when he wore overalls and took his first steps. All this happened without my knowing whether or not I had a master. I was already wearing my

por la casa. Todo esto ocurría sin yo saber si tenía amo o no. Ya yo vestía mi balandrán de carranclán de lista ancha y entraba y salía de la casa sin que nadie me pusiera obstáculos.

Tendría yo algo más de doce años cuando, deseosas de verme, algunas antiguas criadas de la casa hicieron instancias a mi madrina, logrando de ella que me mandase de visita a la casa de mi señora, la Marquesa de Prado Ameno. Fue verificado que un domingo me vistieron de blanco con mi balandrancito de carranclán y pantalones de borlón. Apenas llegué a la casa cuando todas me cargaron, otra me llevaba de la mano acá y allá enseñándome, hasta que me condujeron al cuarto de la señora diciéndole quién era yo. No sé decir lo que pasó; lo cierto es que al día siguiente me envió a buscar mi señora con un criado. Estuve jugando todo el día, mas a la noche, cuando me quería ir a casa de mi amada madrina, no se me llevó. Ella fue a buscarme y yo no fui, qué se yo por qué.

De allí a unos días me hicieron muchos mamelucos de listado cortos y alguna ropita blanca para cuando salía con la librea de paje. Para los días de gala usaba un vestido de pantalón ancho de grana, guarnecido de cordón de oro, chaquetilla sin cuello de raso azul marino, guarnecida de lo mismo, morreón de terciopelo negro galoneado, con plumaje rojo y la punta negra, dos argollitas de oro a la francesa y alfiler de diamante. Con esto y lo demás pronto olvidé mi antigua y recolecta vida. Los teatros, paseos, tertulias, bailes hasta el día y otras romerías me hacían la vida alegre y nada sentía haber dejado la casa de mi madrina, donde sólo rezaba, cosía con mi padrino y, los domingos, jugaba con algunos monifáticos,[11] pero siempre solo, hablando con ellos. A los pocos días tuve por allá a la misma doña Joaquina, que me trataba como a un niño. Ella me vestía, peinaba y cuidaba de que no me rozase con los otros negritos. De la misma mesa, como en el tiempo de la señora la Marquesa de Justiz, se me daba mi plato, que comía a los pies de mi señora la Marquesa de Prado Ameno. Toda esta época la pasaba yo lejos de mis padres.

---

11. "Figura humana o de animales en pintura o de bulto mala y ridículamente hecha" (D. Esteban Pichardo, *Diccionario provincial casi-razonado de vozes cubanas*, 3ª ed. [La Habana: Imprenta y Librería Militar, 1862]) (de aquí en adelante, citamos el título abreviado: *Pichardo*).

cotton cassock with wide stripes and coming and going freely as I pleased.

I was probably a little more than twelve years old when some of the old houseservants, who wanted to see me, asked and convinced my godmother to send me for a visit to the house of my mistress, the Marchioness de Prado Ameno. And so it was that one Sunday they dressed me in my white cotton cassock and embroidered trousers. I had barely reached the house when they all gathered around and one of them took me by the hand, showing me here and there, until they led me to the bedroom, introducing me to the mistress. I do not know how to explain what happened; what I am sure of is that the next day my mistress sent a servant for me. I was playing all day, but that night, when I wanted to go to my dear godmother's home, I was not taken there. She came to pick me up, and, for reasons beyond my comprehension, I did not go.

A few days later they made me several overalls with little stripes and some white clothes for when I went out dressed as a page. For special occasions I wore an outfit with wide, scarlet pants trimmed in gold braid; a short jacket without a collar, made of navy-blue satin adorned the same way; a black velvet cap with a black tip embellished with braid and red feathers; two gold French-style rings; and a diamond pin. With all this and more I soon forgot my old, austere lifestyle. The theater, outings, social gatherings, dances until dawn, and other excursions made my life happy, and I did not at all regret having left my godmother's house, where I only prayed, sewed with my godfather, and on Sundays played with and talked to some crude dolls,[9] but always by myself. After a few days, Doña Joaquina herself came and treated me like a child. She would dress me, comb my hair, and take care that I did not mix with the other black children. Just as in the days of the Marchioness de Justiz, I was given my food from the same table and ate at the feet of my mistress, the Marchioness de Prado Ameno. I spent that entire period far from my parents.

---

9. Painted or stuffed human figures or animals, poorly crafted in caricature (D. Esteban Pichardo, *Diccionario provincial casi-razonado de vozes cubanas*, 3d ed. [Havana: Imprenta y Librería Militar, 1862]) (hereafter cited as *Pichardo*).

Cuando yo tenía doce años ya había compuesto de memoria muchas décimas.[12] Por esta razón mis padrinos no querían que aprendiese a escribir. Yo, sin embargo, se las dictaba de memoria, en particular a una joven morena llamada Serafina. Con estas cartas en décimas manteníamos una correspondencia amorosa.

Desde mis doce años doy un salto hasta la edad de catorce. Paso por alto algunos pasajes en los que se verificaría lo inestable de mi fortuna. Se habrá notado en la relación ya dicha que las épocas no están bien fijadas, ya que era yo demasiado tierno y sólo conservo unas ideas vagas. Como veremos, la verdadera historia de mi vida no comienza sino a partir de 1809,[13] en que empezó la fortuna a desplegarse contra mí hasta el grado de mayor encarnizamiento.

Por la más leve maldad de muchacho me encerraban por veinticuatro horas en una carbonera sin tablas y sin nada con que taparme. Yo era en extremo medroso y me gustaba comer. Como se puede ver todavía, para distinguir un objeto en mi cárcel, en lo más claro del mediodía, se necesitaba una buena vela. Aquí, después de sufrir recios azotes, era encerrado con orden y pena de gran castigo al que me diese siquiera una gota de agua. Tanto se temía en esta casa a tal orden, que nadie, absolutamente nadie, se atrevía, aunque hubiera coyuntura, a darme ni un comino. Lo que en esa cárcel sufrí aquejado del hambre y la sed, y atormentado del miedo.

Era un lugar tan soturno como apartado de la casa, en un traspatio junto a una caballeriza y junto a un apestoso y evaporante basurero, contiguo a un lugar común tan infestado como húmedo y siempre pestífero, separado de él sólo por unas paredes, todas agujereadas, guarida de deformes ratas que sin cesar me pasaban por encima. Yo que tenía la cabeza llena de cuentos de cosas malas de otros tiempos, de las almas aparecidas aquí de la otra vida, y de los encantamientos de los muertos, cuando salía

---

12. Una combinación métrica de diez versos octosílabos, de los cuales, por regla general, rima el primero con el cuarto y el quinto; el segundo, con el tercero; el sexto, con el séptimo y el último; y el octavo, con el noveno.

13. La edición de Franco dice "189." Pero, si calculamos a base de lo que más adelante afirma Manzano: "la amarga vida que he traído desde los trece o catorce años," deberá ser 1809 o 1810.

By the time I was twelve years old, I had already composed several *décimas*[10] by memory. For that reason, my godparents did not want me to learn to read. I, however, dictated the verses from memory, in particular to a young mulatta named Serafina. By means of these letters in verse we maintained an amorous correspondence.

I am jumping ahead from the age of twelve to fourteen. I am passing over some anecdotes that would verify the instability of my fortune. One can see that in all that has been related so far the years are not very precise, for I was too young and only retain vague notions. As we shall see, the true story of my life does not begin until 1809,[11] when destiny began to unleash itself against me with all its fury.

For the least childish mischief, I was locked up for twenty-four hours in a coal cellar without floorboards and nothing to cover myself. I was extremely fearful and liked to eat. As one can still see, in order to distinguish an object in my cell during the brightest midday, a good candle was necessary. Here, after suffering brutal lashes, I was locked up with orders that anyone who might give me even a drop of water was to be severely punished. Such an order was so feared in that house that no one, absolutely no one, dared give me as much as a crumb even if there were an opportunity to do so. What I suffered in that jail is unimaginable, afflicted as I was with hunger and thirst, and tormented by fear.

It was a place as silent as it was removed from the house, in a backyard next to a stable and alongside a stinking, rotting garbage heap, which was near an outhouse, as infested as it was damp, and always foul, separated from me solely by a few hole-ridden walls, which were the lair of deformed rats that incessantly ran over me. Since my head was filled with stories of evil things from other times, of ghostly souls from the afterlife, and of the

---

10. A poem of ten lines in octosyllabic form in which, usually, the first line rhymes with the fourth and the fifth, the second with the third, the sixth with the seventh and the last, and the eighth with the ninth.

11. José L. Franco's edition of *Juan Francisco Manzano, cartas y versos de Juan Francisco Manzano* (Havana: Muncipio de la Habana, 1937) reads "189." If we calculate the date based on information supplied further on by Manzano, the date should be 1809 or 1810: "the bitter life I have had since the age of thirteen or fourteen."

un tropel de ratas haciendo ruido me parecía que estaba aquel sótano lleno de fantasmas.

Yo daba tantos gritos pidiendo misericordia que se me sacaba, pero se me atormentaba de nuevo con tanto fuete[14] hasta más no poder y se me encerraba otra vez, guardando la llave en el cuarto mismo de la señora. En dos ocasiones se distinguió la piedad del señor don Nicolás y de sus hermanos; por la noche me introdujeron un poco de pan bizcocho por una rendija o abertura de la puerta, y con una cafetera de pico largo me dieron un poco de agua.

Esta penitencia era tan frecuente que no pasaba una semana en que no sufriese de este género de castigo dos o tres veces. En el campo tenía siempre igual martirio.

Yo he atribuido mi pequeñez de estatura y la debilidad de mi naturaleza a la amarga vida que he traído desde los trece o catorce años. Siempre flaco, débil y extenuado llevaba continuamente en mi semblante la palidez de un convaleciente con tamañas ojeras.

No es de extrañar que, siempre hambriento, me comiese cuanto hallaba, razón por la que se me miraba como el más glotón. Tan era así, que, como no tenía hora segura para comer, comía a dos carrillos y me tragaba la comida casi entera, de lo que me resultaban frecuentes indigestiones. Estas me obligaban a ir a hacer ciertas necesidades con frecuencia. Todo esto me hacía acreedor de otros castigos. Mis delitos comunes eran: no oír la primera vez que me llamasen y dejar de oír una palabra cuando se me daba un recado.

Como llevaba una vida tan angustiada, sufriendo casi diariamente rompeduras de narices hasta echar por ambos conductos dos caños de sangre; rompedura sobre rompedura, en cuanto me llamaban me entraba un temblor tan grande que apenas podía tenerme sobre mis piernas. No pocas veces sufrí, por la mano de un negro, vigorosos azotes. Como se me suponía esto un fingimiento, no calzaba zapatos sino cuando salía de paje.

Desde la edad de trece a catorce años, la alegría y viveza de mi genio, y lo parlero de mis labios, llamados pico de oro,

---

14. "Voz cubanizada del francés *fouet*. Algunos aplican este nombre a todo instrumento de azotar . . ." (*Pichardo*).

enchantments of the departed, when a troop of rats came out making noise it seemed to me that the cellar was full of ghosts.

I would scream so much, begging for mercy, that they would remove me, but only to punish me anew with as many lashes as their strength permitted, and then I was locked up again with the key kept in the mistress's room. On two occasions, the compassion of Don Nicolás and his brothers was evident; at night they passed a bit of sweet bread through a crack or opening in the door, and, using the long spout of a coffeepot, they gave me a sip of water.

This penance was so frequent that a week did not go by in which I did not suffer this kind of punishment two or three times. In the countryside I always endured the same martyrdom.

I have attributed my short stature and weak constitution to the bitter life I have had since the age of thirteen or fourteen. I was always thin, weak, and emaciated, and my face constantly betrayed the paleness of a convalescent, with enormous rings under the eyes.

Always hungry, it is not surprising that I ate everything I found, and for that reason I was considered an awful glutton. So it was that, since I did not have a customary hour to eat, I would stuff myself and gobble the food down almost without chewing, so I frequently had indigestion. That made me have to take care of certain necessities often. All of this brought on other punishments. My usual offenses were not hearing the first time I was called and missing one word when I was given a message.

Since I led such an anguished life, suffering a broken nose almost daily, to the point that, blow after blow, two streams of blood would pour from my nostrils, as soon as they called me I would be overcome by such intense trembling that my legs could barely support me. More than a few times I suffered vigorous floggings at the hands of a black man. Since it was believed I feigned all this, I did not wear shoes except when I went out as a page.

From the age of thirteen to fourteen, the joy and vivacity of my character and the eloquence of my lips, dubbed the "golden beak," all changed completely into a certain kind of melancholy that, with time, became a personal trait of mine. Music enchanted

se trocó todo en cierta melancolía que se me hizo característica con el tiempo. La música me embelesaba, pero sin saber por qué lloraba, y gustaba de tal consuelo, que cuando hallaba ocasión buscaba la soledad para dar larga rienda a mis pesares. Lloraba, pero no gemía, ni se me añudaba el corazón sino en cierto estado de abatimiento, incurable hasta el día.

Tendría yo unos quince o dieciséis años cuando me llevaron a Matanzas otra vez. Abracé a mis padres y a mis hermanos, y conocí a los que nacieron después de mí. El carácter seco y la honradez de mi padre, como estaban siempre a la vista, me hacía pasar una vida algo más llevadera. No sufría los horribles y continuos azotes ni los golpes de mano que por lo regular sufre un muchacho lejos de algún pariente suyo, aunque siempre mis infelices cachetes y narices estaban. . . .

Cinco años pasamos en Matanzas y era allí mi oficio el amanecer antes que nadie estuviera en pie; barría y limpiaba cuanto podía. Concluida esta diligencia, me sentaba en la puerta de mi señora para cuando despertara que me hallase allí enseguida. Para donde quiera que iba ella, la seguía yo como un falderillo, con mis bracillos cruzados.

Cuando almorzaban o comían, tenía yo cuidado de recoger todo lo que iban dejando. Y tuve que darme maña para engullírmelo todo antes de que se quitara la mesa, ya que en cuanto se paraban había yo de salir tras ellos. Llegada la hora de coser, me sentaba a la vista de mi señora a coser efectos de mujeres, por lo que sé hacer túnicos, camisones, colgaduras, colchones, marcar y coser en holán batista y hacer toda clase de guarniciones.

Llegada la hora de dibujo, que lo enseñaba un ayo que tenían los señoritos don Nicolás y don Manuel, íbamos la señorita doña Concepción, mi señora y yo también. Yo me paraba detrás del asiento de mi señora y permanecía allí todo el tiempo que durara la clase. Todos dibujaban y míster Godfría,[15] que era el ayo, recorría el salón mirando lo que cada persona dibujaba, aquí diciendo esto, allí corrigiendo con el creyón, allá arreglando otra sección. Por lo que yo veía hacer, decir, corregir y explicar me hallé en disposición de contarme por uno de tantos en la clase de dibujo.

---

15. Probablemente "Godfrey."

me, but, without knowing why, I would cry, and enjoyed that relief, so that when I found an opportunity I sought solitude in order to allow my grief free rein. I would cry rather than sob, but I was not faint of heart except during certain states of depression, incurable to this day.

I was probably about fifteen or sixteen when they took me to Matanzas again. I embraced my parents and siblings and met those who were born after me. My father's austere character and integrity, which were always in evidence, made my life somewhat bearable. I did not suffer the horrible, continuous floggings or the beatings that a child far from any relative normally suffers, even though my poor cheeks and nose were always . . .

We spent five years in Matanzas, and my job there was to get up before anyone else; I swept and cleaned all I could. When I finished this assignment, I would sit by my mistress's door so that when she awoke she would find me there right away. Wherever she went, I followed her like a little lapdog, with my skinny arms crossed.

When they lunched or dined, I was careful to pick up everything they left. And I had to be clever to gobble it all up before the table was cleaned off because as soon as they finished I had to follow them out. When the hour for sewing came around, I sat where my mistress could see me sew ladies' things, and thus I know how to make tunics, chemises, draperies, and mattresses, how to mark and sew in fine linen batiste, and how to make all kinds of trimmings.

At the designated time for drawing lessons taught by the tutor for the masters Don Nicolás and Don Manuel, Doña Concepción, my mistress, and I also went. I stood behind my mistress's chair and remained there for the duration of the class. Everyone would draw, and Mr. Godfría,[12] the tutor, walked around the room looking at what each person was drawing, making comments here and there, correcting with a crayon, and touching up parts of the drawings. Because of what I saw done, said, corrected, and explained, I was in a position to consider myself one among many in the drawing class.

---

12. Probably "Godfrey."

No me acuerdo cuál de los niños me dio un lapicero viejo de bronce o cobre y un pedacito de creyón. Esperé a que botasen una muestra y al día siguiente, a la hora de la clase, después de haber visto un poco, me senté en un rincón vuelta la cara para la pared, y empecé a hacer bocas, ojos, orejas, cejas y dientes. Cuando consideraba ser hora de cotejar las muestras con las lecciones ante el director, míster Godfría, yo envolvía mis lecciones, las metía en el seno y esperaba la hora en que se acabasen las dos horas de dibujo. Oyendo y mirando llegué a perfeccionarme. En una ocasión tomé una muestra desechada, pero entera. Aunque no muy perfecta, era una cabeza con su garganta que mostraba una mujer desolada que corría con el pelo suelto, ensortijado y batido por el viento, los ojos saltones y llorosos. La copié tan fielmente, que cuando la concluí, mi señora, que me observaba cuidadosamente haciéndose la desentendida, me la pidió y se la presentó al director. Mr. Godfría dijo que yo saldría un gran retratista y que sería un gran honor para él que algún día retratase yo a todos mis amos.

Desde entonces todos me tiraban muestras de todas clases al rincón del suelo donde yo estaba a medio acostar. Ya cuando estaba bastante aventajado compuse una guirnalda de rosas y otras muchas cosas.

En esta época, tanto como en todas las que serví a mi ama, me iba con ella, que era aficionadísima a la pesca, por las tardes y las mañanas frescas, a buscar qué pescar por la orilla de la parte baja del río de San Agustín que atravesaba por el Molino. Yo le ponía la carnada en el anzuelo y recibía el pez que sacaba. Sin embargo, como la melancolía estaba encentrada en mi alma y había tomado en mi físico una parte de mi existencia, yo me complacía en componer unos versos de memoria, todos tristes, bajo la guásima[16] cuyas raíces formaban una especie de pedestal a los que pescaban. Los versos no los escribía por ignorar este ramo, pero tenía un cuaderno de versos en la memoria e improvisaba cualquier cosa.

---

16. Arbol silvestre.

I do not remember which one of the children gave me an old bronze or copper pencil case and a small piece of crayon. I waited for them to throw away a model design, and the next day, at class time, after having watched a while, I sat in a corner facing the wall and began to draw mouths, eyes, ears, eyebrows, and teeth. When I deemed it to be the moment to compare the sketches with the model designs in front of the teacher, Mr. Godfría, I wrapped up my copies, tucked them into my shirt, and waited for two hours for the drawing lessons to conclude. By listening and watching I came to perfect my skills. On one occasion I took a model that had been thrown out but which was still intact. Though not very perfect, it showed the head and neck of a disconsolate woman, who was running with her hair loose, twisted and whipped by the wind, her eyes bulging and tearful. I copied it so accurately that when I finished, my mistress, who was carefully watching me, though pretending not to, asked me for it and presented it to the teacher. Mr. Godfría said that I would become a great portrait painter and it would be a great honor for him if someday I would paint portraits of all my masters and mistresses.

From then on everyone tossed model designs from all the classes onto the floor in the corner where I was always nodding off. When I was already sufficiently advanced I created a garland of roses and several other things.

At that time, as well as during the entire period in which I was in the service of my mistress, who was very fond of fishing, I would go with her, in the afternoons and the cool mornings, to look for fish downstream in the San Agustín River, which flowed through El Molino Plantation. I would bait the hook and grab the fish that she caught. However, since melancholy took root in my soul and had physically become part of my existence, I took some pleasure in composing verses, all sorrowful ones, by memory under the *guásima* tree[13] whose roots formed a sort of pedestal for those who were fishing. I did not write the verses down since I did not know how to, but I possessed a mental notebook of verses and improvised anything.

13. Wild tree.

Supo mi señora que yo charlaba mucho, ya que los criados viejos de mi casa me rodeaban cuando yo estaba de humor, para gustar de oír mis décimas que, como propio producto de la inocencia, no eran ni divinas ni amorosas, y dio orden expresa en la casa de que nadie me hablase. Nadie sabía explicar el género de mis versos, ni yo me atreví más a decir uno, ya que por dos veces me costó mi buena monda.[17] Como carecía de escritura, para estudiar las cosas que yo componía hablaba solo, haciendo gestos y afecciones según la naturaleza de la composición. Por eso decían que era tal el flujo de hablar que tenía, que por hablar, hablaba con la mesa, con el cuadro, con la pared.

Yo a nadie decía lo que traía conmigo y sólo cuando me podía juntar con los niños les decía muchos versos y les contaba cuentos de encantamientos con sus cantarcitos todos concernientes a la aflictiva imagen de mi corazón, que yo componía de memoria durante el resto del día. Mi ama, que no me perdía de vista ni aun durmiendo, pues hasta soñaba conmigo, hubo de penetrar algo. Una noche de invierno me hicieron repetir un cuento, rodeado de niños y criadas. Mi ama se mantuvo oculta en otro cuarto detrás de unas persianas o romanas. Al día siguiente, por quítame allá esta paja, como suele decirse, enseguida me dieron mi buena monda, me pusieron una gran mordaza y me pararon en un taburete en medio de la sala con unos motes, de los que no me acuerdo, por detrás y por delante. Además, se hizo recta prohibición de que nadie entrara en conversación conmigo y si yo trataba de tenerla con alguno de mis mayores, debían darme un gaznatón.

De noche, a las doce o a la una, debía irme a dormir donde vivía mi madre, que estaba a más de doce cuadras de distancia. Yo, que era en extremo miedoso, tenía que pasar por este trago aun en las noches más lluviosas. Con este y otros tratamientos algo peores, mi carácter se hacía cada vez más taciturno y melancólico. Yo no hallaba consuelo más que recostado en las piernas de mi madre, porque padre de genio seco. . . .

Este se acostaba mientras mi pobre madre y mi hermano Florencio me esperaban hasta la hora que yo viniera. Este último,

---

17. *Dar monda.* Mondar: "Castigar o azotar con exceso." (*Pichardo*)

My mistress found out that I chatted a lot, since when I was in high spirits the old domestic servants gathered around me to enjoy hearing my décimas—which, being the very product of my innocence, were neither spiritual nor amorous—and she gave strict orders for no one in the house to speak to me. No one could explain what kind of verses they were, nor did I dare recite them anymore, because they had already cost me two good beatings. Since I lacked writing skills, in order to study what I was composing I used to talk out loud to myself, affecting gestures and emotions according to the nature of the composition. It was said, therefore, that my facility for expression was such that just to talk, I would talk with the table, with the painting, with the wall.

I did not tell anyone what I was involved in, and only when I was able to join the children did I recite many poems and tell them magical tales with their ditties, all a reflection of the distressing state of my heart and composed by memory during the rest of the day. My mistress, who did not let me out of her sight even when she was sleeping, because she even dreamed about me, must have fathomed what was going on. One winter night, surrounded by children and servants, they made me repeat a story. My mistress hid in another room behind some shades or curtains. The next day, for no good reason at all, as they say, they immediately gave me a thrashing, gagged me, and sat me on a stool in the middle of the parlor with signs I cannot recall, in back and in front of me. It was also strictly prohibited for anyone to enter into conversation with me, and if I tried to converse with any of my elders they were supposed to give me a good throttling.

At night, at about twelve or one, I was to go sleep where my mother lived, more than twelve blocks away. I, who was so very fearful, had to suffer that ordeal even on the rainiest nights. As a result of this and other, worse, treatment, my character became more and more taciturn and melancholy. I only found consolation resting on my mother's legs, because father's sober disposition . . .

He used to go to bed while my poor mother and brother Florencio waited up for me until I arrived. The latter, even if he

aunque estuviera dormido, luego que yo tocaba la puerta y oía mi voz, despertaba y venía a abrazarme. Cenábamos juntos y nos íbamos a la cama.

Unas tercianas que por poco dan conmigo a la sepultura, me privaron de seguir a mi señora a La Habana. Cuando me hallé restablecido enteramente nadie haría en dos años lo que yo en cuatro meses. Me bañaba cuatro veces al día y hasta de noche corría a caballo; pescaba, registré todos los montes, subí todas las lomas, comí cuantas frutas había en las arboledas; en fin, disfruté de todos los inocentes goces de la juventud. En esta época pequeñísima me puse grueso, lustroso y vivo, mas volviendo a mi antiguo género de vida, mi salud se quebrantó y volví a ser lo que era.

Entonces fue cuando recibí una pedrada en la mollera, que me la dio un moreno sin querer. Me llevaron privado a la cama y fue tan riesgosa la herida que, habiéndome abierto o hundido el casco, se me descubría parte del cráneo. La herida me duró abierta más de dos años. Aun todavía por tiempos se me resume. Esta peligrosa herida me fue por mucho tiempo favorable, pues yo era demasiado sanguíneo y de una naturaleza tan débil que la más leve novedad me causaba una impresión que siempre resollaba por aquella parte abierta. Así sucedió que, habiéndome maltratado, yo no sé por qué, todo el padecimiento de aquel acto, unido a tres días que se tardaron en curarme, atrajeron sobre el cráneo una tela negra que fue menester tenaza, hilo y agua fuerte para quemarla.

Era médico de la hacienda entonces don qué sé yo Estorino, un señor a quien yo acompañaba a la caza y a la pesca. Era un hombre tan piadoso como sabio y generoso y que tomó a su cargo mi cura y el cuidado de mis alimentos. Me curaba con sus propias manos hasta llegar al punto de no necesitarse más que tafetán inglés. Le debo esta fineza como otras muchas, muchísimas, por las que le estoy sumamente reconocido. El era el único que sabía mirar mis muchachadas como propios efectos de aquella edad, a lo que unía yo una imaginación traviesa.

Me acuerdo una vez haber pintado una bruja echándole una ayuda a un diablo; aquél tenía el semblante afligido y la bruja risueño. Esta lámina causó a muchos grande risa, pero yo tuve por más de dos meses bastante que llorar, ya que mi padre, con la

was asleep, would wake up when I knocked on the door and he heard my voice, and would run to embrace me. We would eat supper together and go to bed.

A fever that almost killed me prevented me from accompanying my mistress to Havana. When I was fully recovered, nobody could accomplish in two years what I could in four months. I swam four times a day and rode horses even at night; I fished, explored all the hills, climbed all the slopes, ate as much fruit as hung in the groves; in short, I enjoyed all the innocent pleasures of youth. During that very short time, I filled out and became bright and lively; but reverting to my old way of life, my health failed and I returned to what I was before.

That was when I was struck on the head with a rock that a mulatto accidentally threw. I was taken to bed, unconscious; and the wound was so dangerous that, having opened or smashed my skull, a part of my brain was visible. The wound remained open for more than two years. Even now at times it oozes. This dangerous injury was, for a long time, advantageous for I was so apt to bleed and so frail that the slightest change created a sensation in me that always manifested itself in that exposed area. And so it happened, I know not why, that, having been handled roughly, all the pain of that deed, along with the three days it took to cure me, allowed a black membrane to form on my skull, so that it was necessary to burn it off with forceps, thread, and a solution of nitric acid.

Don something-or-other Estorino was the plantation doctor then, a man whom I accompanied hunting and fishing. He was as pious as he was wise and generous, and he took charge of my treatment and cared for my diet. He treated me with his own hands until all that I needed was a court plaster. I am indebted to him for this kindness, and many, many others, for which I am extremely grateful. He was the only one who knew how to view my childish pranks, along with my mischievous imagination, as typical of that age.

I remember one time having painted a witch giving aid to a demon; the latter had a sorrowful look, and the witch was cheerful. This picture prompted much laughter, but I had plenty to cry about for more than two months because my father, with

austeridad de su caracter, me prohibió tomar los pinceles mientras él viviese. Me quitó la cajita de colores y la tiró al río, rompiendo la lámina que le había causado tanta risa.

Como desde que pude hacer algo fue mi primer destino el de paje. Tanto en La Habana como en Matanzas, velaba desde mis más tiernos años más de la mitad de la noche. En La Habana, si no en las noches de teatro, en las tertulias en la casa del señor Marqués de Monte Hermoso o en casa de las señoras beatas de Cárdenas, de donde salíamos a las diez empezaba el paseo después de haber cenado, hasta las once o las doce de la noche. En Matanzas, los días señalados, o no señalados, se comía en casa del señor Conde de Jibacoa o en la del señor don Juan Manuel O'Farrell. Donde quiera que fuese, íbamos a hacer tarde y noche en casa de las señoras Gómez, donde se reunían las personas más conocidas y decentes del pueblo a jugar partido de tresillo, matillo o burro. Yo no me podía separar de detrás del espaldar del taburete de mi ama hasta la hora de partir, que era, por lo regular, a las doce de la noche, hora en que partíamos para el Molino. Si en el ínterim que duraba la tertulia me dormía, o si al ir detrás de la volante, por alguna casualidad se me apagaba el farol (aunque fuese porque los carrilones que dejaban las carretas se llenaban de agua y al caer la rueda saltaba, entrándose por las labores del farol de hojalata), al llegar se despertaba al mayoral o al administrador, y yo iba a dormir al cepo. Al amanecer ejercían éste o aquél sobre mí una de sus funciones,[18] y no como si se tratara de un muchacho.

Pero tanto dominio tiene el sueño sobre el espíritu humano, que no pasaban cuatro o cinco noches cuando era repetido. No me valía nadie, nadie, ni mi pobre madre. Más de dos veces, con mi hermano, les amaneció esperándome, mientras yo, encerrado, esperaba un doloroso amanecer. Ya vivía mi madre tan recelosa, que cuando no llegaba a la hora, poco más o menos, bajaba desde su bohío y se acercaba a la puerta de lo que antes era la enfermería de los hombres, donde estaba el cepo, hacia la izquierda. Por ver si estaba allí me llamaba: "Juan." Yo le contestaba gimiendo y ella decía de afuera: "¡Ay, hijo!" Entonces

---

18. Es decir, la del azote.

his austere nature, prohibited me from taking up my paint brushes as long as he lived. He took away my box of colors and threw it into the river, tearing up the same picture that had made him laugh so much.

From the time when I could first do anything, my destiny was to be a page. In Havana as in Matanzas, from my most tender years, I stayed up more than half the night. In Havana, if not on a night at the theater, at a gathering in the home of the Marquis de Monte Hermoso, or in the home of the pious mistresses Cárdenas, from which we would leave at ten after having dined, the outing would begin and last until eleven or twelve at night. In Matanzas, whether on specified days or others, we ate at the Count of Jibacoa's or at Don Juan Manuel O'Farrell's home. Wherever it might be, we spent the afternoon and evening in the home of the Señoras Gómez, where all the most prominent and honorable people in the town met to play card games—*tresillo, matillo,* or *burro.* I could not budge from the back of my mistress's stool until it was time to depart, which was usually at about twelve midnight, when we left for El Molino. If I fell asleep during the gathering, or if by some chance my lantern went out when I was sitting behind the coachman (even if it was because the deep ruts left by the carts filled with water, which splashed up when the wheels hit them and penetrated the slots in my tin-plate lantern), upon arrival the overseer or the administrator was awakened and I was sent to sleep in the stocks. At dawn, the latter or the former would do a job on me,[14] and not as if I were a child.

But sleep holds such sway over the human spirit that four or five nights did not go by before it happened again. Nobody, absolutely nobody could help me, not even my poor mother. More than twice, daybreak found my mother and brother waiting up for me while I, locked up, awaited a painful dawn. My mother already lived in such apprehension that, when I did not arrive more or less on time, she came down from her shack and approached the door of what used to be the men's infirmary, where the stocks were located to the left. To see if I was there she would call me, "Juan." Sobbing, I would answer her and she would say from outside, "Oh, my son!" Then she would call to her husband from

---

14. The job of administering lashes.

era el llamar de la sepultura a su marido, pues cuando esto ya mi padre había muerto. Tres ocasiones en menos de dos meses recuerdo haber visto repetirse esta escena, como otras en las que me encontraba en el camino. Sin embargo, una de las más memorables para mí fue la siguiente.

Nos retirábamos del pueblo y era ya demasiado tarde. Como venía sentado como siempre, asido con una mano a un barro y en la otra el farol, y como la volante andaba más bien despacio que al paso regular, me dormí de tal modo que solté el farol, pero tan bien, que cayó parado. A unos veinte pasos abrí de pronto los ojos, me hallé sin el farol, vi la luz en donde estaba, me tiré abajo, corrí a cogerlo, antes de llegar di dos caídas con los terrones, tropezando al fin lo alcancé, y quise volar en pos de la volante, que ya me sacaba una ventaja considerable. Pero cuál sería mi sorpresa al ver que el carruaje apretó su marcha, que en vano me esforzaba yo por alcanzarlo y que se me desapareció.

Yo ya sabía lo que me había de suceder. Llorando me fui a pie. Cuando llegué cerca de la casa de vivienda me hallé cogido por el señor Silvestre, que era el nombre del joven mayoral. Al conducirme éste para el cepo, se encontró con mi madre, que, siguiendo los impulsos de su corazón, vino a acabar de colmar mis infortunios.

Ella al verme quiso preguntarme qué había hecho cuando el mayoral, que le imponía silencio, se lo quiso estorbar, sin querer oír ruegos, ni súplicas, ni dádivas; irritado porque le habían hecho levantar a aquella hora, levantó la mano y dio a mi madre con el manatí. Este golpe lo sentí yo en mi corazón. Dar un grito y convertirme de manso cordero en un león todo fue una cosa. Me le zafé con un fuerte tirón del brazo por donde me llevaba y me le tiré encima con dientes y manos.

Cuantas patadas, manotazos y demás golpes que llevé se puede considerar. Mi madre y yo fuimos conducidos y puestos en un mismo lugar. Allí los dos gemíamos al unísono. En el ínterim mis hermanos Florencio y Fernando solos, lloraban en su casa. El uno tendría doce años y el otro cinco. Este último sirve hoy al médico señor don Pintado.

Apenas amaneció cuando dos contramayorales y el mayoral nos sacaron, llevando cada uno de los morenos su presa

the grave, because by then my father had already died. Three times in less than two months, I remember having seen this scene repeated, as well as others in which I found myself as time went by. Among the most memorable for me, however, was the following one.

We were leaving town and it was already very late. Seated as always, hanging onto a bar with one hand and a lantern in the other, and with the coach moving rather more slowly than usual, I fell asleep in such a way that I let go of the lantern but so well that it landed upright. After about twenty paces I suddenly opened my eyes, found the lantern missing, saw the light where it lay, jumped down, and ran to grab it. Before I got to it I fell twice on the rough road, and stumbling, finally reached it, then wanted to fly after the coach, which was already at a considerable distance from me. But how surprised I was to see the carriage accelerate its pace, so that I was exerting myself in vain to catch up to it, and it disappeared from my sight.

I already knew what was to befall me. I walked along, crying. When I drew near the house, I found myself grabbed by Señor Silvestre, the young overseer. As he led me to the stocks, he ran into my mother, who, following her heart, ended up increasing my misfortunes.

Upon seeing me, she tried to ask me what I had done, when the overseer, who demanded silence, endeavored to stop her, refusing to hear of pleas, entreaties, or gifts; irritated because they had made him get up at that hour, he raised his hand and struck my mother with his whip. I felt this blow in my heart. All at once I screamed and was transformed from a gentle lamb into a lion. I wrenched myself loose from his grip with a strong yank of my arm and I attacked him with teeth and fists.

You can imagine how many kicks, punches, and other blows I sustained. My mother and I were led to the same place and locked up. There we moaned in unison. Meanwhile my two brothers, Florencio and Fernando, were crying alone at home. They must have been about twelve and five years old. Today, the latter is in the service of the physician Don Pintado.

It was barely sunrise when the overseer and two of his assistants removed us; each of the mulattos leading his prey to

al lugar de sacrificio. Yo sufrí mucho más de lo mandado, por guapito, pero las sagradas leyes de la naturaleza obraron otra vez con efectos maravillosos.

La culpa de mi madre fue que viendo que el mayoral me tiraba a matar, se le tiró encima y, haciéndose atender, pude ponerme en pie. Llegando los guardieros del tendal[19] nos condujeron, y vi a mi madre puesta en el lugar de sacrificio por primera vez en su vida. Aunque ella estaba en la hacienda, estaba exenta del trabajo como mujer de un esclavo que se supo conducir y hacerse considerar de todos.

Viendo yo a mi madre en este estado, suspenso, no podía ni llorar, ni discurrir, ni huir. Temblaba mientras que, sin pudor, los cuatro negros se apoderaron de ella y la arrojaron en tierra para azotarla. Pedía por Dios. Por ella todo lo resistí. Pero al oír estallar el primer fustazo, convertido en león, en tigre o en la fiera más animosa, estuve a pique de perder la vida a manos del citado Silvestre. Pero pasemos en silencio el resto de esta escena dolorosa.

Pasado este tiempo con otra multitud de sufrimientos semejantes, pasamos a La Habana. Después de un año, sin variar mi suerte en nada, estábamos para partir para Matanzas; era entonces cuando empezaron a rodar las monedas de nuestro católico monarca, el señor don Fernando VII, cuando llegó un mendigo por una limosna. Mi señora me dio para él una peseta de nuevo acuño, pero tan nueva que parecía acabada de fabricar.

El señor don Nicolás me había dado la noche antes una peseta que yo traía en el bolsillo. Tanto vale ésta como la otra, dije yo, y, cambiándola, fui a dar al mendigo su limosna. Me fui a sentar en mi lugar en la antesala cuidando de que mi señora me llamara o necesitara de alguien.[20] De consiguiente saqué la peseta y estaba como el mono, dándole vueltas y más vueltas, leyendo y volviendo a leer sus inscripciones, cuando se me escapó de la mano y cayó al suelo. Como el piso era de hormigón, al caer dio su correspondiente bote, y como estaban entrejuntas la puerta y

---

19. "Cierto espacio de terreno cuadrado, llano solado de hormigón, con sus bordes o muros bajos . . . para poner el café al sol . . ." *(Pichardo)*.
20. El original dice "algien."

the sacrificial site. For being bold, I suffered more than was ordered, but the sacred laws of nature worked again with marvelous results.

My mother's mistake was that she assaulted the overseer when she saw he was about to kill me and, while he was dealing with her, I was able to stand up. When the watchmen arrived from the yard where the coffee beans are dried,[15] they led us away and I saw my mother put in the sacrificial place for the first time in her life. Even though she lived on the plantation, as the wife of a slave who knew how to conduct himself and command respect from everyone, she was exempt from work.

Bewildered, seeing my mother in this position, I could neither cry nor think nor flee. I was trembling as the four blacks shamelessly overpowered her and threw her on the ground to whip her. I prayed to God. For her sake I endured everything. But when I heard the first crack of the whip I became a lion, a tiger, the fiercest beast, and I was about to lose my life at the hands of the aforementioned Silvestre. But let us pass over the rest of this painful scene in silence.

After this period with its multitude of similar torments, we moved to Havana. After a year in which my luck did not change at all, we were about to leave for Matanzas; it was when the coins bearing the likeness of our Catholic monarch, Don Fernando VII, began to be minted, that a beggar came around for alms. For him, my mistress gave me one of the recently issued pesetas, so new that it seemed just minted.

The night before, Don Nicolás had given me a peseta that I had in my pocket. I said to myself, this one is worth as much as the other and, switching them, I proceeded to give the beggar his alms. I went to sit down in my place in the anteroom, attentive in case my mistress should call me or need someone. Then I took out the peseta and, like a monkey, I was turning it over and over again, reading and rereading its inscriptions, when it slipped from my hands and fell to the floor. Since the floor was concrete, the peseta bounced, and because the door and the window abutted each other, the peseta had hardly hit the floor

---

15. A certain square expanse of land, leveled and covered with concrete, with borders or low walls, where coffee beans are dried in the sun (*Pichardo*).

la ventana, no hubo bien caído cuando mi señora salió, me pidió la peseta, se la di, la miró y se puso como una grana. Me hizo pasar por su cuarto a la sala y me sentó en un rincón imponiéndome no me moviese de allí. Para esto ya mi peseta estaba en su poder, conocida por ser la misma suya que me había dado hacía dos minutos.

Estaba la recua del ingenio de Guanabo descargando entonces. Con tales pruebas a la vista, no había duda alguna; esta fatal moneda era la misma que acababa de darme. No se quiso más pruebas. Se sacó la muda de cañamazo, se compró la cuerda y el mulo en que yo debía ir.[21]

Pronto me encontré sobrecogido. Estaba yo en lugar de retención y extrañado de que todos los niños se asomaran a la puerta llorando. Mi señora entraba y salía muy silenciosa, pero diligente. Se sentó y escribió algo. A una le pregunté quedito por mi hermano y supe que estaba encerrado.

Serían cerca de las nueve cuando vi entrar en la sala al negro arriero, de cuyo nombre no me acuerdo ahora. Este se acercó a mí desligando la esquifación,[22] habiendo dejado ya en el suelo una soga de henequén. Yo que esperaba mi común penitencia y viendo el gran peligro que me amenazaba, me escapé por otra puerta, pues la sala tenía tres. Poseído del miedo corrí a mi protector, el señor don Nicolás, y hallé que allí ocultos, tributo propio de la infancia, todos lloraban. La niña Concha me dijo: "Anda a donde está papá."

El señor Marqués me quería bien. Yo dormía con él porque no roncaba y cuando sufría de jaqueca le daba agua tibia y le tenía la frente mientras arrojaba. Si este único mal del que padecía duraba una noche y parte del otro día, yo no faltaba de su cabecera.

En cuanto llegué a su escritorio (todo fue cosa de relámpago), él estaba escribiendo para su ingenio. Me eché a sus pies y, al verme, me preguntó qué había. Se lo dije y me dijo, "¡Gran perrazo! Y ¿por qué le fuiste a robar la peseta a tu ama?" "No

---

21. Es decir, a trabajar en el ingenio de Guanabo.
22. "Voz generalmente usada en la parte occidental para significar el vestuario de los negros que trabajan en el campo" *(Pichardo)*.

when my mistress came out and asked me for the coin. I gave it to her; she looked at it and turned scarlet. She had me pass through her room to the drawing room and sat me in a corner, forbidding me to move from that spot. My peseta was already in her possession, and she knew it was the same one she had given me two minutes before.

The mule team from the Guanabo sugar mill was unloading then. In the light of such evidence, there could be no doubt; this fatal coin was the same one she had just given me. No further proof was necessary. A change of burlap clothes was brought out, and the rope and mule were bought for my departure.[16]

Suddenly I found myself frightened. I was confined, and wondered why all the children appeared at the doorway crying. My mistress was coming and going silently but diligently. She sat down and wrote something. I quietly asked someone about my brother and found out that he was locked up.

It must have been about nine when I saw the black muleteer, whose name I do not now remember, come into the room. Having already left a henequen rope on the floor, he approached me, unfolding plantation workers' clothes.[17] Expecting my customary punishment and seeing the impending danger that threatened me, I escaped through another door of the three in the room. Possessed by fear, I ran to my protector, Don Nicolás, and found everyone cowering there like babies, crying. The little girl, Concha, said to me, "Go to papa."

The marquis loved me very much. I slept with him because he did not snore, and when he had migraines I would give him warm water and hold his head while he vomited. If this sole illness from which he suffered lasted all night and part of another day, I never left his bedside.

When I reached his study (everything happened like a flash of lightning), he was writing to his sugar mill. I threw myself at his feet, and upon seeing me he asked me what was going on. I told him and he said to me, "Scoundrel! Why did you steal the

---

16. To work at the Guanabo sugar mill.
17. In Western Cuba this refers to the clothing worn by the slaves who worked in the countryside.

señor," repliqué yo, "el niño me la dio." "¿Cuándo?" me preguntó. "Anoche," le contesté.

Subimos todos arriba. Le preguntaron al niño, mostrándole la moneda, y él contestó que no.

La verdad es que la turbación mía no me dejó hacer una cabal relación que aclarase un hecho tan evidente. Una pregunta, cien amenazas, el aspecto de las esquifaciones, un ingenio tan temido en aquellos días por causa de su mayoral, un tal Simón Díaz, cuyo nombre sólo infundía terror en la casa cuando con él amenazaban, todo se acumuló en mi corta edad de dieciseis años y yo no supe ya responder, sino rogar y llorar.

El señor Marqués intercedió y por lo pronto me condujeron a mi calabozo. Cuatro días con sus noches estuve allí sin ver el término de mi arresto. Por fin, al quinto día, como a las seis de la mañana, abrieron la puerta. En todo este tiempo no me alimentaba sino con lo que mi hermano y algún otro me daban por debajo de la puerta.

Sacado fuera se me vistió mi esquifación, se trajo la cuerda nueva y, sentado sobre una caja de azúcar, esperaba el momento en que todos estuviéramos reunidos para partir por mar para Matanzas con todo el equipaje.

Mi hermano, al pie de la escalera, me miraba con los ojos lacrimosos e inflamados. Tenía debajo del brazo un capotillo viejo que yo tenía y su sombrerito de paja. El no había cesado de llorar desde que supo mi destino. Eramos tal en amarnos que no se dio el caso de que comiese una media naranja sin que yo tomase igual parte. Yo hacía lo mismo. Comíamos, jugábamos, salíamos a cualquier mandado y dormíamos juntos. Así esta unión, vinculada por los indisolubles lazos del amor fraterno, se rompió. No así como otras veces por algunas horas, sino por algo más de lo que yo ni nadie se atrevió a imaginar.

Por fin toda la familia estaba lista. Se me ató para conducirme como el más vil facineroso. Estábamos en la puerta de la calle cuando nos hicieron entrar. La señorita doña Beatriz de Cárdenas, hoy madre Purita en el convento de monjas Ursulinas, fue la mediadora para que no se viese sacar de su casa en tal figura a uno a quien todos tendrían compasión, pues era un niño.

peseta from your mistress?" "I did not, sir," I replied. "The master gave it to me." "When?" he asked. "Last night," I answered.

We all went upstairs. They asked the master, showing him the coin, and he answered "No."

The truth is that my confusion did not allow me to tell a coherent story in order to explain such an obvious incident. A question, a hundred threats, the appearance of the plantation clothing, a sugar mill so dreaded in those days because of its overseer, a certain Simón Díaz, whose name alone caused terror in the house when it was used as a threat—all of that heaped onto my scarce sixteen-year-old shoulders so that I did not know how to respond except to plead and cry.

The marquis intervened, and for the present they took me to my prison cell. I was there four days and nights, with no end to my arrest in sight. Finally, on the fifth day at about six in the morning, they opened the door. During this whole time I ate only what my brother and some other boy slipped under the door.

Once outside, I was dressed in my plantation workers' clothes, the new cord was brought, and, seated on a box of sugar, I awaited the moment when we would all be gathered together with all the luggage to set out by sea for Matanzas.

From the foot of the stairway, my brother stared at me with teary, red eyes. Under his arm he held one of my old capes and his little straw hat. He had not stopped crying since he found out about my fate. We loved each other so much that he never ate half an orange without my taking the other half. I would do likewise. We used to eat, play, run errands, and sleep together. Thus this union, bound by the indissoluble bonds of fraternal love, was broken. Not just for a few hours as on other occasions, but for much more than I or anyone else dared imagine.

Finally the whole family was ready. I was tied up to be led away like the vilest criminal. We were in the front doorway when we were ordered to come inside. Doña Beatriz de Cárdenas, now Mother Purita in the convent of the Ursuline nuns, acted as intermediary, so that a being for whom everyone would have compassion because he was a child might not be seen removed from her house in such a state.

Me desataron los brazos y una de las criadas, contemporánea, amiga y paisana de mi madre, me ató un pañuelo a la cabeza. Como yo no usaba ni calzado ni sombrero, no tuve más que buscar. Salimos y nos embarcamos en la goleta de la que era patrón don Manuel Pérez. Nos hicimos a la vela y en pocas horas navegábamos para Matanzas.

Tardamos, no sé por qué, dos días. Al siguiente, al amanecer, dimos fondo en el puerto a donde íbamos.

En cuanto llegamos, mi hermano se dio prisa en echarse al bote conmigo. Durante la navegación me dio una muda de ropa mía que había cogido al salir. Me mudé en cuanto llegamos a bordo, pues aquel traje, puesto por primera vez en mi vida, nos hacía a los dos el mismo efecto.

Así que llegamos a tierra con el resto de la familia, como éramos pequeños y no teníamos equipaje, debíamos irnos todos para la casa del comandante del Castillo, el señor don Juan Gómez, a quien se le dirigían cartas con órdenes acerca de la familia. Nosotros, que no sabíamos nada de esto, de una parte, y por el deseo de ver a nuestra madre, por otra, cuando entramos por la calle del medio, en la segunda bocacalle, doblamos con disimulo y, tomando la calle del Río nos enderezamos a paso largo para el Molino.

Como se me había desatado y como en todo este tiempo no se me había ni mirado ni preguntado por aquel traje en que fui sacado y, además, porque en mi conciencia de nada me culpaba, iba alegre, a paso largo para llegar a los brazos de mi madre. La amaba tanto que siempre pedía a Dios me quitase primero la vida a mí que a ella. No me creía yo con bastante fuerza para sobrevivirla.

Al fin llegamos. Le hicimos un corto cumplimiento al administrador, Mr. Denny, y sin decirle casi nada, sino que el resto de la familia venía detrás, picamos hasta dar con nuestra madre. Los tres abrazados de pie formábamos un grupo. Mis tres hermanos más chicos nos rodeaban abrazándonos por los muslos. Mi madre lloraba y nos tenía estrechados contra su pecho. Daba gracias a Dios porque le concedía la gracia de volver a vernos.

No habíamos pasado más de tres minutos en esta actitud, cuando de repente llegó a la puerta el moreno Santiago, sirviente

They untied my arms, and one of the maids, who was a friend of my mother's from her hometown, tied a handkerchief around my head. Since I wore neither shoes nor hat, I had nothing else to pack. We left and boarded the schooner, whose skipper was Don Manuel Pérez. We set sail and, in a few hours, were on our way to Matanzas.

I do not know why the voyage took us two days. On the third day, at sunrise, we anchored at our port of destination.

As soon as we arrived my brother hurried to jump into the skiff with me. During the voyage he gave me a change of my clothes that he had grabbed upon leaving. I changed clothes as soon as we got on board, for that other outfit, worn for the first time in my life, had the same effect on both of us.

Thus we arrived on shore with the rest of the family, and, since we were young and did not have baggage, we were all to go to the house of the commander of the Castillo, Don Juan Gómez, to whom were addressed the letters with orders concerning the family. In part because we did not know anything about this and also because we wanted to see our mother, when we entered the main street we furtively turned down the second cross street and hurriedly took River Street straight toward El Molino Plantation.

Because I had been unbound and during all this time I had not been watched or asked about that outfit in which I was taken away, and besides, because to my mind I was guilty of nothing, I hastened along, merrily, eager to reach my mother's arms. I loved her so much that I always prayed to God to take my life before hers. I did not believe that I had enough strength to survive her.

We finally arrived. We briefly paid our respects to the administrator, Señor Denny, telling him only that the rest of the family was following, and we went on until we found our mother. The three of us stood hugging each other, forming a group. My three younger brothers surrounded us hugging our legs. My mother was crying and held us tightly to her bosom. She was thanking God for allowing her the favor of seeing us again.

We had not spent more than three minutes in that position when suddenly the mulatto Santiago, a houseservant,

de la casa, agitado, bañado en sudor y colérico. Sin saludar a la que lo vio nacer y la que lo libró de que mi padre le sacudiese el polvo muchas veces en sus días de aprendizaje, echó una grumentada[23] que nos sobrecogió a todos. Me dijo sin el menor reparo, "Sal pa' afuera, que desde el pueblo he venido corriendo dejándolo todo al diablo. ¿Quién te mandó venir?" "¿Y quién me dijo que me esperara?," le dije yo con una especie de rabia creyendo que esto era cosa suya, y no juzgando el tamaño de mi mal.

Mi madre me agarró por el brazo y le preguntó qué había hecho yo. "Ahora lo sabrá," contestó, y sacando la misma cuerda de La Habana me ató y condujo para el tendal, donde ya me esperaba un negro, a quien se me entregó. Tomamos el camino del ingenio de San Miguel y llegamos a él alrededor de las once. A todas estas yo estaba en ayunas. Abrió[24] la carta que se le había enviado de La Habana. Con mucha dificultad consiguió un par de grillos para mí. Como estaba yo tan delgado costó mucho trabajo cerrarlos; se usaron unas rocas, pero después, para quitármelos, fue menester limarlos.

Por las cartas dirigidas al señor comandante, yo debía de haber sido traído a este lugar con un comisionado por el camino de Yumurí, pero por la prisa que nos dimos resultó esto otro.

Veinticinco[25] de mañana y otros tantos de tarde por espacio de nueve días, cuartos de prima y de madrugada[26] fue el castigo recomendado en la carta. Me interrogó el mayoral. Le dije la verdad lisa y llana. Por primera vez vi clemencia en este hombre de campo. No me castigó. Yo me aplicaba en todos los trabajos y me esforzaba cuanto podía con tal de no llevarme los veinticinco. Todos los días me parecía que había llegado mi hora.

Al cabo de quince días me mandaron buscar sin ser menester tener padrinos.[27]

---

23. Palabra enigmática. ¿Será "grumetada" de "grumete"?
24. Manzano no nos dice quién, pero suponemos que fue el mayoral.
25. Azotes.
26. El trabajo de la "negrada" en el ingenio se dividía en cuatro partes. El "cuarto de prima" correspondía al período desde la puesta del sol hasta medianoche; el de "madrugada," desde el alba hasta mediodía, generalmente en el campo.
27. Intermediarios o protectores.

appeared at the door, agitated, drenched in sweat, and angry. Without greeting the woman who witnessed his birth and who, during his formative years, saved him many times from my father's thrashings, he let loose with a cuss[18] that took us all by surprise. He told me without the slightest hesitation, "Get out of here. I've come running like the devil all the way from town. Who told you to come here?" "And who told me to wait?" I retorted angrily, misjudging the gravity of my situation, while thinking that all this was just Santiago's doing.

My mother grabbed me by the arm and asked him what I had done. "You'll soon find out," he answered, and, taking out the same cord from Havana, he tied me up and led me to the yard where the coffee beans are dried, where he handed me over to a black who was waiting for me. We took the road to the San Miguel sugar mill and arrived there around eleven. I was in the dark about all that. He[19] opened the letter that had been sent to him from Havana. With great difficulty he found a pair of shackles for me. As I was so thin, it was very hard to close them; some rocks were used, but later, in order to remove them, it was necessary to file them off.

According to the letters sent to the commander, I was to have been brought to this place by a deputy by way of the Yumurí road, but because of our haste the result was different.

The punishment recommended in the letter was twenty-five[20] in the morning and some more in the afternoon for a period of nine days, and work from dusk to midnight and sunrise to noon.[21] The overseer interrogated me. I told him the plain and unadorned truth. For the first time, I saw compassion in this man from the countryside. He did not punish me. I applied myself to all tasks and made a supreme effort so as not to suffer the twenty-five lashes. Every day it seemed my hour had come.

At the end of two weeks, they sent for me without intermediaries.

---

18. This word is a puzzle. Could it be *grumetada*, from *grumete* (a sailor's cuss word)?
19. Manzano does not say who, but we assume it was the overseer.
20. Lashes.
21. The work of the slave on the sugar plantation and mill was divided into four parts. The *cuarto de prima* corresponded to the period from dusk to midnight; the *madrugada* lasted from sunrise to noon, generally in the fields.

Anteriormente me aconteció un lance muy semejante a éste. Vivíamos en el pueblo, frente a la iglesia, en la casa del facultativo, el señor Estorino. Mi señora me mandó a cambiar una onza con el señor don Juan de Torres, el hijo. Fui yo para traerla. Cuando llegué me mandaron poner el dinero, que era menudo y pesetas, sobre una de las mesitas de caoba que estaban preparadas para el tresillo en el gabinete. Al cabo de algún rato tomó mi señora el cambio sin contarlo.

Como yo tenía por oficio cada media hora tomar el paño y sacudir todos los muebles de la casa, tuvieran polvo o no, fui a hacerlo. Al tomar una mesa por una de las medias hojas que abrían y cerraban, una peseta que había caído en la abertura de medio saltó al suelo y sonó al dar yo con el paño. Mi ama, que estaba en el cuarto siguiente, al oír el ruido salió. Me preguntó por aquella moneda y yo le dije lo que había ocurrido. Contó entonces su dinero y lo halló de menos. Tomó la moneda sin decirme palabra.

Todo aquel día se pasó sin la menor novedad. Sin embargo, al día siguiente, como a las diez, se apareció el mayoral del ingenio San Miguel. Me hizo atar codo con codo y, saliendo por delante, nos encaminamos hacia el ingenio. Entonces supe que mi ama sospechaba que yo hubiese introducido la moneda en la rendija que formaba la desunión de las dos hojas de la mesita porque quería quedarme con ella.

El mayoral, de cuyo nombre y apellido no me acuerdo, se apeó al llegar a la calle del Río, en la esquina opuesta a la medio fabricada casa del señor don Alejandro Montoro, entonces cadete de milicias de Matanzas. Entramos en una fonda que allí había. Pidió de almorzar para él y para mí y me consoló diciéndome que no tuviera cuidado.

Me desató primero y mientras yo comía, él hablaba con otro hombre también de campo. Me acuerdo que le dijo, "Su pobre padre me ha suplicado lo mire con caridad. Yo también tengo hijos."

Al cabo de algún rato nos levantamos. El me montó detrás en el aparejo y llegamos al ingenio. Estuve sentado toda la tarde en el trapiche de abajo. Me mandó de comer lo que él comía y por la noche me entregó a una vieja que por su mucha

Previously, an event very similar to this one happened to me. We were living in town across from the church in the house of the physician Señor Estorino. My mistress sent me to Don Juan de Torres Jr. to get change for a coin. I went to get it. When I came back, they told me to put the money, which was small change and pesetas, on one of the little mahogany tables set up for playing tresillo in the study. A while later my mistress took the change without counting it.

Since it was my duty to take a cloth every half hour and dust all the furniture in the house, whether or not it was dusty, I went off to do so. As I grasped one of the two leaves that opened and closed on a table and dusted it with my rag, a peseta, which had fallen into the crack, bounced onto the floor and made a noise. My mistress, who was in the next room, came rushing out when she heard the noise. She asked me about that coin and I told her what had happened. She then counted her money and saw that it was a peseta short. She took the coin without saying a word to me.

That whole day went by without incident. The next day at about ten, however, the overseer from the San Miguel sugar mill showed up. He ordered that I be tied up like a prisoner, and took the lead as we walked toward the sugar mill. Then I discovered that my mistress suspected that I had placed the coin in the crack between the two leaves of the table because I wanted to keep it for myself.

The overseer, whose name I do not remember, dismounted upon arriving at River Street, on the corner opposite the half-constructed house of Don Alejandro Montoro, a military cadet in Matanzas at that time. We went into an inn around there. He ordered lunch for himself and for me and consoled me, saying not to worry.

He untied me first, and while I was eating he talked to another peasant. I remember that he said to him, "His poor father has begged me to look after him kindly. I have children, too."

After a while we got up from the table. He sat me behind him in the saddle and we arrived at the sugar mill. I sat all afternoon in the sugar mill below. He sent me the same food that he ate and at night placed me in the care of an old woman

edad no salía al trabajo. Allí estuve cosa de nueve a diez días, al cabo de los cuales me mandó a buscar mi ama, sin que yo sufriese el menor quebranto.

En esta época vivía mi padre, pues fue él y algún otro criado quienes me preguntaban y examinaban acerca de lo que había sucedido y yo les contestaba. Pero mi ama nunca creyó sino que era algún ardid de que me valía. Yo creo, sin embargo, que el tratamiento que allí tuve fue disposición de ella. Mi pronta vuelta y el caso omiso que hizo el mayoral de mí siendo tiempo de molienda me lo hacen creer así. Este paso me sucedió en tiempos en que estuvo en España el señor don José Antonio y fue la primera vez que vi un ingenio.

Después de ésta se sucedieron una multitud de sinsabores, todos sin motivos justos. Un día de flatos era para mí señales de una tempestad. Y los flatos eran tan frecuentes que no podría enumerar los increíbles trabajos de mi vida. Me basta con decir que desde que tuve bastante conocimiento, hasta poco después de la primera constitución de 1812, cuando me arrojé a una fuga, no hallo un solo día que no esté marcado con algún percance lacrimoso para mí. Saltando por encima de varias épocas, dejo atrás una multitud de lances dolorosos. Me ceñiré únicamente a los más esenciales como fuente o manantial de otras mil tristes vicisitudes.

Me acuerdo que una vez que se me había roto las narices, como se tenía de costumbre casi diariamente, se me dijo, "Te he de matar antes de que cumplas la edad." Esta palabra, para mí tan misteriosa como insignificante, me causó tanta impresión, que al cabo de unos días le pregunté a mi madre. Ella, admirada, me lo preguntó dos veces más y me dijo, "Más puede Dios que el demonio, hijo." No me dijo nada más que satisfaciese mi curiosidad. Ciertos avisos de algunos criados antiguos de mi casa nativa y de mis padrinos, todos unánimes, algunos con variaciones, me han dejado alguna idea de esta expresión.[28]

En otra ocasión me acuerdo que, no sé por qué pequeñez, iba a sufrir. Pero un señor, para mí siempre bondadoso que me apadrinaba como era de costumbre, dijo, "Mire Ud., que éste

---

28. Alusión, sin duda, a su posible libertad al alcanzar la mayoridad.

who, because of her advanced age, did not go to work. I was there for about nine or ten days without my suffering the slightest harm, at the end of which my mistress sent for me.

At that time my father was alive, and it was he and another servant who asked and interrogated me about what had happened, and I answered them. But my mistress chose to believe that it was another one of my tricks. I think, however, that the good treatment I received there was the result of her orders. My rapid return and the overseer's ignoring me during the milling season prompt me to believe so. This incident happened to me during the period in which Don José Antonio was in Spain, and it was the first time I saw a sugar mill.

After this incident a multitude of troubles ensued, all without justification. A day of indisposition was for me the sign of a storm. And indispositions were so frequent that I could not enumerate the incredible travails of my lifetime. Suffice it to say that ever since I was first aware of things up until shortly after the first Constitution of 1812, when I became a runaway, I cannot find a single day that is not marked for me with some tearful incident. Skipping over several years, I will leave behind a multitude of painful episodes. I will limit myself solely to the most essential ones as fountain or wellspring of a thousand other sorrowful vicissitudes.

I remember how once when my nose had been broken, as customarily happened almost daily, I was told, "I'm going to kill you before you come of age." This phrase, for me as mysterious as it was insignificant, made such an impression on me that after a few days I asked my mother about it. Shocked, she asked me to repeat the words two more times and told me, "God is more powerful than the devil, son." She told me nothing else that would satisfy my curiosity. Certain information with few variations held alike by some of the old servants from my birthplace and from that of my godparents, has left me with some idea of what this expression means.[22]

On another occasion I recall that I was going to suffer for I do not know what triviality. But a gentleman, who was always kind to me and who acted as my godfather, as was customary,

---

22. Doubtless an allusion to his possible freedom upon reaching legal majority age.

va a ser más malo que Rousseau y Voltaire, y acuérdese Ud. de lo que yo le digo." Esta fue otra expresión que me hacía andar averiguando quiénes eran estos dos demonios. Cuando supe que eran unos enemigos de Dios me tranquilicé. Desde mi infancia, mis directores me habían enseñado a amar y a temer a Dios. Llegaba hasta tal punto mi confianza que, pidiendo al cielo suavizase mis trabajos, me pasaba casi todo el tiempo de la prima noche. Rezaba cierto número de padrenuestros y Ave Marías a todos los santos de la corte celestial, todo para que al día siguiente no me fuese tan nocivo como el que pasaba. Si me acontecía uno de mis comunes y dolorosos apremios, lo atribuía solamente a mi falta de devoción o enojo de algún santo que había echado en olvido para el día siguiente. Todavía creo que ellos me depararon la ocasión y me custodiaron la noche de mi fuga de Matanzas para La Habana, como veremos. Pues yo tomaba el almanaque y todos los santos de aquel mes eran rezados por mí diariamente.

Como he dicho, vivíamos en la casa del señor Estorino, quien sabía algo de dibujo. Pintaba yo decoraciones en papel, hacía mis bastidores de güines de cañas[29] cimarronas o cujes de yayas,[30] hacía figuras de naipes y de cartón y daba entretenimiento a los niños con grandes funciones de sombras chinescas, a las que concurrían algunos niños y niñas del pueblo hasta las diez o más de la noche. Hoy son grandes señores y no me conocen. Hacía títeres que parecían que bailaban solos. Eran de madera que yo formaba con un tajo de pluma y que pintaban los hijos del señor don Félix Llano, señor don Manuel y don Felipe Puebla, señor don Francisco Madruga, el farruco, y otros. Otros, como el señor José Fontón, meneó las orejas delante de mí; me propuse yo también menearlas, y lo conseguí, suponiendo la causa. Entonces fue cuando el señor don Beranés, descubriendo en mí los primeros síntomas de la poesía, me daba lo que llaman pie forzado[31] y cuando versaba en la mesa me echaba, a hurtadillas, alguna

---

29. *Güin:* varilla de la familia de las cañas.
30. *Cujes de yayas:* vara flexible. Viene de "cuje" (arbusto que se usaba con frecuencia para hacer látigos) y "yaya" (árbol silvestre, delgado y flexible) (*Pichardo*).
31. Entre los decimistas, darle una frase al improvisador de décimas, quien está obligado a incorporarla en el último verso del poema.

said, "Look here, this one is going to be worse than Rousseau and Voltaire. Remember what I am telling you." This was another expression that made me go around trying to find out who those two devils were. When I found out that they were enemies of God, I was relieved. From childhood, my elders had taught me to love and fear God. My confidence was such that I would spend almost all the early hours of the evening praying to heaven that my labors be alleviated. I would recite a certain number of Lord's Prayers and Hail Marys to all the saints of the celestial court, all so that the next day would not be as injurious as the one before. If one of the usual painful punishments befell me, I would attribute it solely to my lack of devotion or the ire of some saint whom I had forgotten in my prayers for the following day. I still believe that they provided me with the opportunity the night I fled from Matanzas for Havana and watched over me, as we shall see. For I took the almanac with me, and every day I prayed to all the saints in it.

As I have mentioned, we lived in Señor Estorino's house, and he knew quite a bit about drawing. I painted paper ornaments, made my frames from sticks of wild cane or lancewood,[23] cut figures from playing cards and cardboard, and entertained the children with grandiose Chinese shadows shows, which were attended by some boys and girls from town and lasted until ten at night or later. Today they are important ladies and gentlemen and no longer know me. I used to make puppets that seemed to dance by themselves. They were made of wood carved with my penknife and were painted by the children of Don Félix Llano, Don Manuel and Don Felipe Puebla, Don Francisco Madruga the Spaniard, and others. Still others, like Don José Fontón, wiggled his ears for me; I, too, decided to wiggle mine and succeeded, by figuring out how to do it. That was when Don Beranés, discovering in me the early signs of a poet, would challenge me, as they say, with the final line of a décima,[24] and when he composed

---

23. These refer to narrow, flexible branches from wild bushes, which were frequently used to make whips.
24. Among poets, a challenge to improvise by supplying the last verse line of the décima.

mirada sin que mi señora lo penetrara. A más de suplicárselo yo, él tenía bastante confianza en la casa y sabía lo estirado que yo andaba.

Esto mismo me sucedía con el padre Carrasedo, con don Antonio Miralla y con don José Fernández Madrid, todos en diferentes épocas.

Si tratara de hacer un exacto resumen de la historia de mi vida, sería una repetición de sucesos todos semejantes entre sí. Desde mi edad de trece o catorce años, mi vida ha sido una consecución de penitencia, encierro, azotes y aflicciones. Así determino describir los sucesos más notables que me han acarreado una opinión tan terrible como nociva. Sé que nunca, por más que me esfuerce con la verdad en los labios, ocuparé el lugar de un hombre perfecto o de bien. Pero a lo menos ante el juicio sensato del hombre imparcial, se verá hasta qué punto llega la preocupación del mayor número de los hombres contra el infeliz que ha incurrido en alguna flaqueza.

Pero vamos a saltar desde los años de 1810, 11 y 12 hasta el presente de 1835, dejando en su intermedio un vastísimo campo de vicisitudes, escogiendo de él los graves golpes con que la fortuna me obligó a dejar la casa paterna o nativa para probar las diversas cavidades con que el mundo me esperaba para devorar mi inexperta y débil juventud.

En 1810, si mal no recuerdo, yo era el falderillo de mi señora. Se puede decir así, porque era mi obligación seguirla siempre, a menos que fuese a sus cuartos, porque entonces me quedaba a las puertas impidiendo la entrada a todos, o llamando a quien llamase, o haciendo silencio si consideraba que dormía.

Una tarde salimos al jardín largo tiempo. Ayudaba a mi ama a recoger flores o a trasplantar algunas maticas como género de diversión. Mientras tanto, el jardinero andaba por todo lo ancho del jardín cumpliendo con su obligación. Al retirarnos, sin saber materialmente lo que hacía, cogí una hojita, una hojita no más de geranio donato. Esta malva, sumamente olorosa, iba en mi mano, mas ni yo sabía lo que llevaba. Distraído con mis versos de memoria, seguía a mi señora a una distancia de dos o tres pasos. Iba tan ajeno de mí, que iba haciendo añicos la hoja, de lo que resultaba mayor fragancia. Al entrar en una antesala, no sé

verses at the table he would glance at me furtively without my mistress's grasping his meaning. Despite my pleas, he was well trusted in the house and knew how vulnerable I was.

The same thing happened to me with Father Carrasedo, with Don Antonio Miralla, and with Don José Fernández Madrid, all at different stages of my life.

If I were to try to give a precise summary of the story of my life, it would be a repetition of events, all similar. From the age of thirteen or fourteen I have experienced penance, confinement, lashes, and misfortunes. So I have decided to describe the most noteworthy events that have occasioned such terrible and harmful opinions of me. I realize that, no matter how much I try to speak the truth, I will never take my place as a perfect or even honorable man. But at least, in the eyes of the prudent judgment of impartial men, one will see to what extremes the prejudice of the majority touches the unfortunate being who has become the victim of some weakness.

But let us jump from 1810, 1811, and 1812 to 1835 in the present, omitting a vast array of vicissitudes between those dates and choosing from them the harsh blows of fate that forced me to leave my paternal home or birthplace in order to experience the varied abysses in the world waiting to devour my inexpert and fragile youth.

In 1810, if I am not mistaken, I was my mistress's lapdog. One can say this because it was my duty to always follow her, except into her rooms, and then I was to remain at the door, keeping everyone out or calling whomever she requested, or demanding silence if I thought she was sleeping.

One afternoon we went out to the garden for quite a while. I was helping my mistress pick flowers or transplant little bushes as a kind of entertainment. Meanwhile the gardener was walking all around the garden fulfilling his responsibilities. As we were leaving, without knowing exactly what I was doing, I picked a leaf, nothing more than a small leaf from a geranium. Unaware of what I was doing, I held that extremely fragrant plant in my hand. Distracted by the verses consigned to my memory, I was walking two or three steps behind my mistress. Unconscious of what I was doing, I tore the leaf to shreds, which produced an even stronger aroma. As she entered one of the anterooms, my

con qué motivo, retrocedió mi ama. Hice paso, pero al enfrentarse conmigo le llamó la atención el olor. Colérica de pronto, con una voz vivísima y alterada, me preguntó, "¿Qué traes en las manos?" Yo me quedé muerto. Mi cuerpo se heló de inmediato y, sin poder apenas tenerme, del temblor que me dio en ambas piernas, dejé caer la porción de pedacitos en el suelo.

Se me tomaron las manos, se me olió y tomándose los pedacitos fue un montón, una mata y un atrevimiento de marca. Se me rompieron mis narices y enseguida vino el administrador, don Lucas Rodríguez, emigrado de Santo Domingo, a quien se me entregó.

Serían las seis de la tarde y era en el rigor del invierno. La volante estaba puesta para partir para el pueblo. Yo debía seguirlos. Pero cuán frágil es la suerte del que está sujeto a continuas vicisitudes. Yo nunca tenía hora segura y esta vez se verificó, como en otras muchas, como veremos.

Yo fui para el cepo. En este lugar, antes enfermería de hombres, cabrán, si existe aún, cincuenta camas en cada lado. Aquí se recibían a los enfermos de la finca, además de los del ingenio San Miguel. Ahora estaba vacía y no se le daba ningún empleo. Allí estaba el cepo y sólo se depositaba en él algún cadáver hasta la hora de llevarlo al pueblo a darle sepultura. Allí, puesto de dos pies, con un frío que helaba, sin ninguna cubierta, se me encerró. Apenas me vi solo en aquel lugar cuando me parecía que todos los muertos se levantaban y vagaban por todo lo largo del salón. Una ventana medio derrumbada que caía al río o zanja cerca de un despeñadero ruidoso que hacía un torrente de agua, golpeaba sin cesar. Y cada golpe me parecía un muerto que entraba por allí de la otra vida. Considerad ahora qué noche pasaría.

No bien había empezado a aclarar cuando sentí correr el cerrojo. Entró un contramayoral, seguido del administrador. Me sacaron una tabla parada a un horcón que sostiene del colgadizo un mazo de cujes, como cincuenta de ellos. Vi al pie de la tabla al administrador envuelto en su capote. Dijo debajo del pañuelo que le tapaba la boca, con voz ronca, que se me amarraran las manos. Las ataron como las de Jesucristo. Me cargaron y metieron los pies

mistress drew back, for what reason I do not know. I stepped aside, but upon coming face to face with me she noticed the fragrance. Suddenly angered, she asked me in a sharp, upset tone of voice, "What do you have in your hands?" My body immediately froze; barely able to stand up because both my legs were trembling, I dropped the handful of shredded leaves on the floor.

She grabbed my hands, smelled them, and picked up the pieces, which became a pile, a bush, an outstanding audacity. My nose was shattered, and I was handed over to the administrator who immediately showed up, Don Lucas Rodríguez, an emigrant from Santo Domingo.

It must have been about six in the afternoon, and it was the worst part of the winter. The coach was set to leave for town. I was to follow them. But how fragile is the fate of he who is subject to continuous mishaps. My life was never predictable, and this time, like many others, would confirm this, as we shall see.

I was sent to the stocks. If it still exists, in that place, which was once an infirmary for men, about fifty beds would fit on each side. Here is where the sick on the plantation were received, along with those from the San Miguel sugar mill. At that time it was empty and not functioning as an infirmary. That is where the stocks were, and only some cadavers were stored there until it was time to carry them to town to be buried. There, forced to remain standing, frozen by the cold and with nothing to cover me, I was locked up. I was scarcely alone in that place when it seemed that all the dead were rising and wandering up and down the length of that room. A broken-down shutter banged incessantly out over the river or ditch, near a noisy torrent of water falling from a cliff. And each blow seemed to be a dead person who was entering through the window from the afterlife. Imagine what kind of night I must have spent.

No sooner had the first light of day appeared when I heard the lock turn. An assistant overseer entered, followed by the administrator. They took out a board, propped up against a beam that supports a bunch of hoop-poles for tobacco, about fifty of them, hanging from the roof. At the foot of the board I saw the administrator wrapped in his cloak. From under the handkerchief that covered his mouth, in a husky voice, he ordered my hands to be tied. They were tied like Jesus Christ's. They lifted me and

en las dos aberturas que tenía. También mis pies se ataron. ¡Oh, Dios! Corramos un velo por el resto de esta escena. Mi sangre se derramó. Yo perdí el sentido, y cuando volví en mí me hallé en la puerta del oratorio en los brazos de mi madre, anegada en lágrimas.

Esta, a instancias del padre don Jaime Florit, se retiró desistiendo del intento que tenía de ponérsele delante qué sé yo con qué pretensión. A las nueve o poco más que se levantó mi señora, fue su primera diligencia averiguar si se me había tratado bien. El administrador, que la esperaba, me llamó y me le presentó. Ella me preguntó si quería otra vez tomar unas hojas de su geranio. Como yo no quise responder, por poco me sucede otro tanto y tuve que decir que no.

Serían cosa de las once cuando me entró un crecimiento. Se me puso en un cuarto. Tres días sin intermisión estuve en este estado. Me daban baños y untos. Mi madre no venía allí sino por la noche, cuando se consideraba que estuviesen en el pueblo. Al sexto día, cuando ya se contaba con mi vida, andaba yo algún poco. Era cosa de las doce cuando me encontré con mi madre, que atravesaba por el tendal. Me encontró y me dijo, "Juan, aquí llevo el dinero de tu libertad. Ya tú ves que tu padre se ha muerto y tú vas a ser ahora el padre de tus hermanos. Ya no te volverán a castigar más. Juan, cuidado he. . . ." Un torrente de lágrimas fue mi única respuesta y ella siguió. Yo fui a mi mandado. Mas el resultado de esto fue que mi madre salió sin dinero y yo quedé a esperar qué sé yo qué tiempo que no he visto llegar.

Después de este pasaje me aconteció otro y es el siguiente. Estando en el Molino, trajeron del ingenio unas cuantas aves, capones y pollos. Como yo estaba siempre de centinela del que llegaba, me tocó, por desgracia, recibirlas. Entré la papeleta, dejando las aves en el comedor o pasadizo debajo de la glorieta que se hallaba a la entrada. Leyeron el papel y se me mandó llevarlo al otro lado para entregárselo a don Juan Mato, que era mayordomo o celador de aquella otra parte. Lo tomé todo despidiendo al arriero, e iba contento, pues en este intervalo respiraba yo. Entregué lo que recibí y me acuerdo que eran tres capones y dos pollos.

placed my feet into two openings in the board. My feet were also tied. Dear God! Let us draw a curtain over this scene. My blood was shed. I lost consciousness, and when I came to I found myself in the doorway of the oratory chapel in the arms of my mother, overwhelmed with tears.

On Father Don Jaime Florit's counsel, she left, forsaking the plan she had to intercede for I do not know what purpose. At nine or a little after, my mistress awoke, her first concern was to verify if I had been treated well. The administrator, who was expecting her, called me and presented me to her. She asked me if I wanted to take some leaves from her geranium again. As I refused to respond, I came very near being punished again, so I finally had to answer "No."

It must have been about eleven when I began to swell. I was put in a room. For three days, without respite, I was in that state. They bathed me and applied ointments. My mother did not visit me there except at night, when she thought the others were in town. On the sixth day, when I was no longer in a life-threatening state, I walked about a bit. It was about noon when I came upon my mother, who was crossing the drying yard. She found me and said, "Juan, I have here the money for your freedom. You see, your father has died and you are now going to be the father of your brothers. They will no longer punish you. Juan, be careful, I have . . ." A stream of tears was my only response, and she cried, too. I went about my work. But the result of all this was that my mother ended up with no money and I was left to await some uncertain time that has yet to come.

After this episode, the following event occurred. When I was at El Molino, some birds—capons and chickens—were brought from the sugar mill. As I was the one who always looked out for visitors, it unfortunately fell to me to receive them. I took the delivery receipt inside, leaving the birds in the dining room or corridor, under the little bower located at the entrance. They read the receipt and ordered me to take it to the other side of the plantation to deliver it to Don Juan Mato, who was the steward or watchman over there. I took everything from the muleteer, dismissing him, and was content, since in the interim I took a breather. I handed over what I had been given, and I remember that they were three capons and two chickens.

Pasadas unas dos semanas o algo más, fui llamado para que diese cuenta de un capón que faltaba. Al momento dije que habían venido tres y dos pollos y que eso había sido lo que yo había entregado. Quedó esto así. Mas a la mañana siguiente vi venir al mayoral del ingenio. Habló largo rato con mi señora y se fue. Servimos el almuerzo y cuando yo iba a meterme el primer bocado en la boca, aprovechando el momento . . . me llamó mi ama. Me mandó que fuese a casa del mayoral y le dijese qué sé yo qué cosa. Aquello me dio mal ojo. Se me oprimió el corazón y fui temblando. Como yo estaba acostumbrado, por lo regular, a irme a entregar yo mismo, de este modo, iba receloso.

Llegué a la puerta y estaban los dos, el de la finca y el antes dicho. Le di el recado y, haciéndose el sordo, me dijo, "Entra, hombre." Como me hallaba en caso de estar bien con estas gentes, porque a cada rato caía en sus manos, le obedecí. Iba a repetir el recado cuando el señor Domínguez, que así era el apellido del mayoral del ingenio, me cogió por un brazo diciendo "A mí es a quien busca." Sacó una cuerda de cáñamo delgada, me ató como a un facineroso, se montó a caballo y, echándome por delante, me mandó correr.

Nos alejamos de aquellos contornos con prontitud. Era con el fin de que ni mi madre, ni mi segundo hermano, ni los niños y niñas me viesen, porque todos al momento llorarían y la casa sería un punto de duelo o me apadrinarían. Nos habíamos alejado como un cuarto de legua, cuando, fatigado de correr delante del caballo, di un traspié y caí. No bien había dado en tierra cuando dos perros o dos fieras que le seguían se me tiraron encima. El uno metiéndose casi toda mi quijada izquierda en su boca, me atravesó el colmillo hasta encontrarse con mi muela. El otro me agujereó un muslo y la pantorrilla izquierda, todo con la mayor voracidad y prontitud. Estas cicatrices están perpetuas, a pesar de los veinticuatro años que han pasado. El mayoral se tiró del caballo sobre los perros y los separó. Mi sangre corría en abundancia, principalmente en la pierna izquierda, que se me adormeció. Me agarró por la atadura con una mano, echando una retahila de obscenidades. Este tirón me descoyuntó el brazo

Some two weeks or more had passed when I was called to give an account of a missing capon. Right away I said that there had been three plus two chickens and that had been what I had delivered. This was all there was to it. But the next morning I saw the overseer from the sugar mill approaching. He spoke a long while with my mistress and then left. We served lunch, and when I was going to take the first bite, savoring the moment . . . my mistress called me. She told me to go the overseer's house and tell him I do not remember what. That gave me a bad feeling. My heart raced and I went, trembling. Since normally I was accustomed to turning myself in, so it was that I went with great misgivings.

I arrived at the door, and both of them were there, the plantation overseer and the aforementioned person. I gave him the message, and, ignoring it, he told me, "Come in, boy." As I was in the habit of getting on well with these people, since I fell into their hands so often, I obeyed him. I was going to repeat the message when Señor Domínguez, that was the name of the overseer from the sugar mill, grabbed me by the arm, saying, "He is looking for me." He took out a rope made of flimsy hemp, tied me up like a criminal, mounted his horse, and, pushing me ahead, ordered me to run.

We quickly distanced ourselves from that neighborhood so that neither my mother, nor my second brother, nor the other boys or girls would see me, because they would all immediately cry, the house would become a sorrowful place, and they would protect me. We had gone about a fourth of a league when, tired of running in front of the horse, I tripped and fell. No sooner had I hit the ground than two dogs or two beasts, which were following him, attacked me. One of them, holding my entire left cheek in his mouth, sank his fang all the way through to my molar. The other one perforated my thigh and my left calf, with the utmost voracity and speed. These scars persist in spite of the twenty-four years that have transpired since then. The overseer leaped from the horse onto the dogs and separated them. I was bleeding profusely, especially from my left leg, which fell numb. He grabbed me with one hand by the rope that bound me, hurling a stream of obscenities at me. This yank dislocated my right arm,

derecho, del que aún no he sanado. En tiempos revueltos padezco en él de ciertos dolores como gotoso.

Caminando como pude, llegamos al ingenio. Dos ramales con sus rocas me fueron puestas. Se me curaron las mordidas qué sé yo con qué unto, y fui para el cepo. Llegó la noche fatal. Toda la gente estaba en hila; se me sacó al medio un contramayoral, el mayoral y cinco negros. Me rodearon a la voz de "Tumba."[32] Dieron conmigo en tierra sin la menor caridad, como quien tira un fardo que nada siente, uno a cada mano y pie y otro sentado sobre mi espalda. Se me preguntaba por el pollo o capón. Yo no sabía qué decir, pues nada sabía. Sufrí veinticinco azotes. Decía mil cosas diferentes, pues se me mandaba a decir la verdad y yo no sabía cuál. Me parecía que al decir que me lo había hurtado cumplía y cesaría el azote, pero había que decir qué había hecho con el dinero y era otro aprieto. Dije que había comprado un sombrero. "¿Dónde está el sombrero?" Era falso. Dije que compré zapatos; no hubo tal. Dije, y dije y dije tantas cosas por ver con qué me libraba de tanto tormento.

Nueve noches padecí este tormento; nueve mil cosas diferentes decía al decirme "di la verdad" y azotarme. Ya no tenía qué decir. Algo que lo pareciese para que no me castigasen. Pero no porque yo tal cosa supiera.

Acabada esta operación iba a arrear bueyes de prima o de madrugada, según el cuarto que me tocaba. Todas las mañanas iba una esquela[33] de lo que había dicho en la noche. Al cabo de diez días, el lunes, esparcida la voz por todo el ingenio, ya se sabía a fondo la causa de aquel género de castigo, cuando el arriero Dionisio Covadonga (que era el arriero) se presentó al mayoral y le dijo que no se me castigase más, porque el buscado capón o pollo se lo había comido el mayordomo don Manuel Pipa.

---

32. En *Los negros esclavos* nos dice Ortiz que "se llamó 'tumbadero' el sitio destinado habitualmente para la pena de azotes, donde los esclavos se 'tumbaban' o 'viraban' para que sobre sus espaldas el látigo marcara el rigor de la represión esclavista" (p. 246).
33. A la señora.

which has not yet healed. In bad weather I suffer certain pains like those of gout.

Walking as well as I was able, we arrived at the sugar mill. I was tied with two ropes fastened around two rocks. My bite wounds were cured with some kind of ointment, and I was placed in the stocks. The fatal night arrived. All the people formed a line; an assistant overseer, the overseer, and five blacks pulled me out into the middle. Around me they shouted, "Drop."[25] They mercilessly threw me on the ground, as one throws a sack that has no feelings, one holding down each hand and foot and another seated on my back. They asked me about the chicken or capon. I did not know what to say because I knew nothing about it. I suffered twenty-five lashes. I said a thousand different things because they were demanding I tell the truth and I did not know which truth they wanted. I thought that saying I had taken it would suffice and the whipping would stop, but then I would have to say what became of the money, so I found myself in another dilemma. I said that I had bought a hat. "Where is the hat?" It was a lie. I said I had bought shoes; there were none. I said so many things, over and over again, trying to see how to free myself from so much torture.

I suffered these torments for nine nights; I said nine thousand different things as they shouted at me, "Tell the truth!" and whipped me. I no longer had anything left to say, anything that it seemed might end their punishing me. But not because I knew such things.

When this business was finished, I would go to drive oxen at night or in the morning, depending on which shift fell to me. Every morning a note[26] was sent about what I had said the night before. After ten days, on Monday, the news spread through the entire sugar mill, and finally the reason for such punishment was known. Then the muleteer, Dionisio Covadonga (who was the muleteer), appeared before the overseer and told him not to punish me any further because the capon or chicken in question had been eaten by the steward, Don Manuel Pipa. The day he

---

25. In *Los negros esclavos*, Ortiz tells us that *tumbadero* was the place habitually destined for punishment by flogging; the slaves threw themselves on the ground (*tumbar*) so that the whip would mark the harsh stamp of slavery's oppression on their backs (246).
26. To the mistress.

El día que él le dio las aves para que las condujese por la tarde al Molino con la papeleta, se le quedó un pollo capón en la cocina, sin advertirlo. A las once de la noche, cuando él volvió del pueblo conduciendo las raciones del día siguiente, lo vió. Por la mañana avisó al mayordomo, no creyendo sino que fuese alguno que lo había hurtado y escondido en su bohío que era la cocina. Este le dijo que era de los que él debió haber llevado al Molino, mas no obstante esto, lo tomó y lo dejó en su cuarto. Al día siguiente su cocinera se lo guisó.

Se llamó y se interrogó a la morena Simona. Declaró ser cierto. Dijo el mayoral que por qué no habían hablado antes. Dionisio dijo que nadie sabía, pues sólo se oía decir que capón, capón, pero sin saber cuál era, y que si no le hubiera contado yo a la Simona y al Dionisio cuál era el buscado capón, nadie hubiera comprendido.

No sé si se dio parte de este asunto, pero lo cierto es que desde aquel día cesó el castigo. Se me puso con un gran garabato a aflojar bagazo[34] seco y a apilarlo para que lo condujeran en las canastas a las hornallas.

En este día me tocó, como uno de tantos, ir a cargar azúcar para la casa de purga.[35] Como no podía andar se me quitó una roca, y todas se me hubieran quitado si no temieran que me fugara.

Estaba yo metiendo hormas en uno de los tinglados, hacia la izquierda. Acababa de soltar la horma y de haber dado unos pasos cuando parecía que se desplomaba el firmamento detrás de mí. Era un gran pedazo del techo con unas cuantas viguetas que se derrumbó detrás de mí cogiendo al negro Andrés, criollo. Yo, con el susto, caí por una abertura debajo de la casa de purga. Mi guardiero gritaba, toda la negrada voceaba. Acudieron a sacar a Andrés, y yo me salí como pude por la parte baja de la puerta.

---

34. *Bagazo:* residuo de la caña después de serle extraído el jugo o guarapo, empleado como combustible.

35. *Casa de purga:* "Fábrica grande, aunque muy baja por los extremos para cerrarlos de modo que el edificio queda casi oscuro, sin corriente de aire; el piso de madera está horadado con agujeros, en que entran las *Hormas* hasta su mitad: aquí se echa el barro y se deja el tiempo suficiente para que purgue el azúcar por los *Furos*, destilando la *Miel*, que recibe abajo un tinglado a propósito" (*Pichardo novísimo*).

gave the birds to Dionisio so he could take them with the message that afternoon to El Molino, unbeknownst to Don Dionisio, one capon chicken remained behind in the kitchen. At eleven that night, when he returned from town with the rations for the next day, he saw it. The next morning he told the steward, believing only that someone had stolen it and hidden it in his hut, which was the kitchen. The steward told him that it was one of the ones that were to have been taken to El Molino, but in spite of this, he took it and left it in his room. The next day, his cook prepared it for him.

The mulatta, Simona, was called and questioned. She declared everything to be true. The overseer asked why they had not said anything before. Dionisio said that nobody knew because all that one heard was talk about some capon or other, but nobody knew which capon, and if I had not told Simona and Dionisio which was the capon in question, nobody would have understood.

I do not know if this matter was reported, but the fact is that from that day on the punishment stopped. I was assigned to loosen up the dry bagasse[27] with a hook and to pile it up for transport in baskets to the ovens.

During those days it fell to me, as to many others, to carry sugar to the filtering house.[28] Since I was unable to walk, they took off one of the rocks; they would have cut all of them loose if they did not fear that I would run away.

I was putting the sugarloaf cones in one of the sheds toward the left. I had just released one of the cones and taken a few steps when it seemed as if the sky was falling down behind me. It was a huge piece of the roof with several beams that fell behind me, hitting the black Creole, Andrés. From the shock, I fell through an opening down under the filter house. My watchman was shouting; all the slaves were yelling. They rushed to help Andrés out, and I got myself out the best I could through the

---

27. The crushed, juiceless remains of sugarcane as it comes from the mill, often used as fuel in the mill.
28. The filtering house was a large, low building with a dark, almost airless interior. The wooden floor contained holes into which were placed the large, conical filters. Clay in the filters aided in distilling the liquid from the sugar, which passed through the holes in the floor into channels and receptacles (*Pichardo novísimo*).

Sacaron al antes dicho con mil trabajos, y tenía todo el cráneo roto, el pellejo del cerebro arrollado, los ojos reventados. Lo condujeron al Molino y murió a pocas horas.

A la mañana siguiente, aún no había el aire disipado bien la neblina, cuando vi aparecerse al niño Pancho, hoy señor don Francisco de Cárdenas y Manzano. Yo estaba débilmente en mi ejercicio de aflojar y apilar bagazo cuando se me presentó, seguido de mi segundo hermano, el cual me insinuó que venía por mí. El cambio de traje y de fortuna fue todo uno. Cuando llegó[36] el desgraciado a quien las vigas maltrataron, se divulgó que yo estuve a pique de perecer también, por lo que mi hermano, que servía al niño Pancho, alcanzó que éste pidiese a su madre por mí, y lo consiguió sin la menor dificultad. Tuve que venir a pie una legua de camino bastante escabroso y el señorito se adelantó en su jaca. Cuando llegamos, mi hermano y el niño me presentaron a la señora, mi ama, la que por primera vez vi que me trató con compasión. Me mandó para el interior de la casa. Mi corazón estaba tan oprimido que no quería ver ni la comida, que era para mí la más sagrada y precisa atención.

Caí en una tristeza tal que ni viendo a todos los muchachos enredados en juegos, ni porque me llamaban, salía de mi triste abatimiento. Comía poco y casi siempre llorando. Por este motivo se me mandaba limpiar las caobas, para que no estuviese llorando o durmiendo. Toda mi viveza desapareció, y como mi hermano me quería tanto, se hizo común entre ambos este estado. El no hacía más que estarme consolando, pero este consuelo era llorando conmigo.

Por este motivo ya no se me llevaba al pueblo detrás de la volante. Todos caían sobre mí para hacerme jugar y yo no salía de mi melancólico estado.

Entonces me dedicaron a dormir con el niño Pancho y mi hermano en un cuarto. Me compraron sombrero y zapatos, cosa para mí muy nueva. Se me mandaba bañar y a paseos por la tarde. Iba a las pescas y a cazar con un señor.

---

36. Al Molino.

bottom section of the door. They extricated him with a great deal of effort; his whole skull was crushed, the skin on his head was scraped off, his eyes popping. They took him to El Molino, where he died a few hours later.

The next morning the haze had not yet completely dissipated when I saw the young master Pancho, who is now Don Francisco de Cárdenas y Manzano, approaching. I was feebly carrying out my duty of loosening and piling up the bagasse when he turned up, followed by my second brother, who hinted that he was coming for me. My change of outfit and luck happened all at once. When the unfortunate slave who had been maimed by the beams arrived,[29] the news spread that I, too, had been in danger of perishing, and so my brother, who was in the service of young master Pancho, urged him to speak to his mother on my behalf, and, without the slightest difficulty, the young man did so. I had to travel on foot one league on a very rugged road, and the young master went ahead on his pony. When we arrived, my brother and the young master brought me to my mistress, my owner, whom I saw treat me with compassion for the first time. She sent me inside. My heart was so troubled that I could not even stand the sight of food, which was for me the most sacred and essential kindness.

I sank into such a depression that I did not emerge from my sorrowful despondency, even when I saw all the children engrossed in games or when they called to me. I ate very little and was almost always in tears. That is why I was ordered to clean the mahogany furniture, so I would not be crying or sleeping. All my liveliness disappeared, and since my brother loved me so much this condition was shared by both of us. He did nothing else but console me, but did so by crying with me.

For this reason I no longer rode to town behind the coachman. Everyone pestered me, trying to make me play, but I did not shrug off my melancholy state.

Then they allowed me to sleep in the same room with master Pancho and my brother. They bought me a hat and shoes, something totally new for me. They made me bathe and

---

29. At El Molino.

Pasado algún tiempo vinimos para La Habana y se me dejó con el señor don Nicolás que me quería, no como a esclavo, sino como a un hijo a pesar de su corta edad. Entonces se me fue disipando aquella tristeza inveterada en mi alma y se me declaró un mal de pecho con una tos medio espasmódica que me curó el señor don Francisco Luvián. El tiempo disipó, ayudado de mi juventud, todos mis males. Estaba bien tratado, mejor vestido y querido. Tenía casaca que me mandaba hacer mi nuevo amo; tenía muchos reales y era mi oficio recoser toda su ropa, limpiar sus zapatos, asearle su cuarto y darle de vestir. Como este señor desde bien joven observó unas costumbres perfectas e irreprensibles, quería que todo lo que estuviese a su alcance fuera lo mismo. Sólo me privó de la calle, de la cocina y del roce con personas de malas costumbres. Conseguí nunca recibir de él ni la más leve reconvención. Lo quería sin tamaño.

Apenas aclaraba y lo veía puesto en pie, le preparaba antes de todo la mesa, sillón y libros para que se entregase al estudio. Me fui identificando de tal modo con sus costumbres que empecé yo también a darme estudios. En todos los trámites de mi vida, la poesía, ya próspera, ya adversa me suministraba versos análogos a mi situación. Tomaba sus libros de retórica y me ponía mi lección de memoria. La aprendía como el papagayo y ya creía que sabía algo. Sin embargo, conocía el poco fruto que le sacaba a aquello, pues nunca tenía ocasión de darle uso. Entonces determiné darme algo más útil, que fue el aprender a escribir.

Este fue otro apuro. No sabía cómo empezar. No sabía cortar pluma y me guardé de tomar ninguna de las de mi señor. Sin embargo, compré mi tajaplumas, plumas, y papel muy fino y con algún pedazo de papel de los que mi señor botaba, escrito de su letra, lo metía entre llana y llana[37] con el fin de acostumbrar el pulso a formar letras. Iba siguiendo la forma de lo que tenía debajo. Con esta invención antes de un mes ya hacía renglones

---

37. Plana.

take walks in the afternoon. I went fishing and hunting with a gentleman.

After some time, we went to Havana and I was left in the service of Don Nicolás, who loved me, not as a slave, but as a son, notwithstanding his young age. That sadness, rooted so deeply in my soul, began to dissipate then; but I was diagnosed with a chest disease and a somewhat spasmodic cough, which Don Francisco Luvián cured. Time, aided by my youth, drove off all my ailments. I was well-treated, better-dressed, and more loved. I had a coat that my new master had ordered made for me, and I had many *reales*. It was my duty to mend all his clothes, clean his shoes, tidy up his room, and arrange his clothing for him. Because this gentleman observed proper and irreproachable habits since his early years, he wanted everything within reach to be just so. He only forbade my going out alone, entering the kitchen, and mixing with indecent people. I never received even the slightest reprimand from him. My affection for him knew no bounds.

At daybreak when I saw him arise, I would prepare his desk, chair, and books before anything else, so he could devote himself to his studies. I began identifying with his habits so thoroughly that I, too, began my own study regimen. Throughout all the stages of my life, poetry—sometimes happy, sometimes sorrowful—afforded me verses in harmony with my situation. I used his rhetoric books and learned my lesson by heart. I learned it like a parrot and even believed that I knew something. However, I recognized how few were the fruits of my labor, since I never had the opportunity to use the information. It was then that I decided to dedicate myself to something more useful, learning to write.

That was another problem. I did not know how to start. I did not know how to cut quills and refrained from taking any from my master. I, nevertheless, bought myself a penknife, quills, and very fine paper, which I placed over a discarded sheet[30] written in my master's hand in order to accustom myself to the feel of fashioning letters. I worked along tracing the shapes on the paper below. With this method, in less than a month I could already

---

30. The original says "entre llana y llana" for *plana*, indicating a page of paper.

MIMÉTISM

logrando la forma de letra de mi señor. Por eso hay cierta identidad entre su letra y la mía.

Contentísimo con mi logrado intento me pasaba desde las cinco hasta las diez ejercitando la mano en letras menudas. Aún de día, cuando tenía tiempo, lo hacía también. Me ponía al pie de algún cuadro cuyos rótulos fueran de letras mayúsculas. Con muchos rasgos logré imitar las letras más hermosas. Llegué a tenerlas entonces que más parecían grabadas que de pluma.

El señor marqués me encontró una vez y por lo que me dijo acerca de ella llegué a creer que ya sabía escribir. Entonces supo mi señor por los que me veían desde las cinco en mi tren de escritura, que yo pasaba todo el tiempo embrollado con mis papeles. No pocas veces me sorprendió en la punta de una mesa que había en un rincón. Me impuso dejase aquel entretenimiento como nada correspondiente a mi clase y que buscase que coser. En este punto no me descuidaba porque siempre tenía alguna pieza entre manos. Para ganar se me prohibió la escritura, pero en vano. Todos se acostaban y entonces encendía mi cabito de vela y me desquitaba a mi gusto copiando las más bonitas letrillas de Arriaza[38] a quien imitaba siempre. Me figuraba que con parecerme a él ya era poeta o sabía hacer versos. Me pillaron una vez algunos papelitos de décimas y el señor don Coronado fue el primero que pronosticó que yo sería poeta, aunque se opusiera todo el mundo. Supo cómo aprendí a escribir y con qué fin, y aseguraba que con otro tanto han empezado los más.

En tanto que esto hacía, mi señor estaba en vísperas de enlazarse con la señorita doña Teresa de Herrera y yo era el mercurio que llevaba y traía[39] (pero por supuesto ya ella estaba pedida). Este distinguido lugar me lucraba mucho, pues tenía doblones sin pedir. Tantos que no sabía qué hacer con el dinero, y después de hacer gran provisión de papel, pluma, bonito tintero, buena tinta y regla de caoba, lo demás se lo enviaba a mi madre en efectivo.

---

38. Juan Bautista Arriaza y Supervilla (1770–1837), poeta neoclásico y traductor del *Arte poético* de Boileau.
39. Recados o cartas.

write lines that imitated my master's handwriting. For that reason there are certain similarities between his penmanship and mine.

Very happy with my successful experiment, I spent from five to ten o'clock practicing my hand at making small letters. Even during the day, when I had time, I also practiced. I would station myself at the foot of some painting whose title was in capital letters. With many strokes I was able to imitate the most beautiful letters. I succeeded then in making them look more like engravings than handwriting.

The marquis discovered me one time, and from what he said even I believed that I already knew how to write. Then my master found out, from those who used to see me in the act of writing from five on, that I was spending all my time engrossed in my papers. More than a few times he caught me at the head of a table that was in a corner. He ordered me to abandon that pastime, which did not correspond to my class, and to look for something to sew. As for sewing, I would take care to always have some at hand. So as not to interfere with my productivity, I was prohibited from writing; but it was in vain. For when everyone went to bed, I would light my candle stump and indulge myself, copying the prettiest verses from Arriaza,[31] whose writing I always imitated. I figured that if my writing looked like his, I was already a poet or knew how to compose verses. Once they got hold of some scraps of papers full of décimas, and Don Coronado was the first to predict that I would be a poet, even though everyone was against it. He found out how I learned to write and why, and confirmed that most had begun the same way.

Meanwhile, my master was on the verge of marrying Doña Teresa de Herrera, and I was the messenger who went back and forth[32] (but of course he had already asked for her hand in marriage). This distinguished position was very lucrative for me because I received doubloons without asking for them—so many of them that I did not know what to do with the money, and after stocking up on paper, quills, a beautiful inkwell, good ink, and a mahogany ruler, I sent the rest in cash to my mother.

---

31. Juan Bautista Arriaza y Supervilla (1770–1837), neoclassic poet and translator of Boileau's *Art poétique*.
32. With messages or letters.

Pasamos a Guanajay con motivo de la temporada que los señores condes de Jibacoa hacen todos los años. Allí a mi futura ama no le quedaron favores que no me prodigara. Como la primera costura que me enseñó mi señora fue la de mujeres, al lado de la señora Dominga, mujer blanca y su costurera, tuve el gran honor de costurar en algunos túnicos de mi señorita.

Ya sabía y sé de guarniciones, colchones, colgaduras de cama, cosía en holanes y sabía hasta marcar en holán de cambray, lo que me era muy celebrado en obsequio de la fina educación que me dio mi ama. Entre mil contentos pasé todo el tiempo que duró la correspondencia hasta que serví las bodas y fui su paje de librea cuando salían a paseo y a misa. Con esta ama mi felicidad iba cada día en más aumento. Hacía que se me guardase en el número de su familia las más pulidas consideraciones y mi señor por lo tanto la imitaba viéndome esmerarme en darle gusto en el cumplimiento de mis obligaciones.

Esta felicidad fue cosa de un poco más de tres años. Cuando vino mi señora, la de Matanzas, oyó la fama de mis servicios en toda clase, y sin saber yo por qué, determinó llevarme consigo otra vez. Era tal mi agilidad, principalmente en la asistencia de enfermos, así tan chiquitillo como parecía en mi edad de 18 años, que se me pedía prestado en la familia cuando había algún enfermo de velarse, como sucedió esta vez.

Asistía al señor don José Ma. de Peñalver, que estaba de cuidado por un dolor que padecía. Yo no sólo sabía templar el baño, darle la bebida a tiempo, ayudarle a levantar para ciertas diligencias sin apretones, y enjugarle cuando se bañaba, sino que en toda la noche no pegaba mis ojos. La pasaba en vela, con el reloj delante, tintero y papel, donde hallaba el médico, por la mañana, un apunte de todo lo ocurrido en la noche; hasta las veces que escupía, roncaba, sueño tranquilo o inquieto le informaba. El señor don Andrés Ferriles, el doctor don Nicolás Gutiérrez y otros al verme asistir a enfermos me celebraron este orden que he seguido en muchas ocasiones.

Yo estaba, como dije, asistiendo al señor don José María cuando vino mi señora que impulsada de tantos elogios me insinuó la determinación que había hecho, con mucho cariño. Yo

We moved to Guanajay, for it was the season of the year that the Count and Countess of Jibacoa always spend there. There my future mistress lavished me with every possible favor. Since the first stitch my mistress taught me was for women's clothing, I had the great honor of sewing some of my mistress's camisoles, at the side of her white seamstress, Señora Dominga.

I already knew, and know now, all about trim, mattresses, and bed curtains, could sew on batiste, and even knew how to embroider names on cambric, a much celebrated skill, owing to the refined instruction my mistress gave me. I spent the courtship days in the utmost happiness, until I served during the wedding ceremony and was the page when they went out for a ride or to mass. In the service of the mistress, my happiness increased with every passing day. She insisted that I be treated well among the members of her family, and my master, therefore, followed her lead, seeing how I took great pains to please her in the performance of my duties.

This good fortune lasted for a little more than three years. When my mistress, the one from Matanzas, heard about my reputed services of all kinds, she decided, without my knowing why, to take me back with her again. Although I appeared small for my eighteen years, my capabilities were such, especially in the care of the ill, that I was borrowed by families when there was someone sick to watch over, as was the case on this occasion.

I attended Don José María de Peñalver, who needed care for a pain he was suffering. Not only was I able to warm up his bathwater, give him a beverage on schedule, gently help him get up to take care of certain necessities, and dry him off when he bathed, but also I kept vigil during the entire night. I stayed awake with a clock, an ink well, and paper in front of me, on which the doctor, in the morning, would find a record of everything that happened during the night; it even informed him of how many times he spit and snored, and whether he slept soundly or poorly. Upon seeing me assist the sick, Don Andrés Ferriles, Dr. Nicolás Gutiérrez, and others have praised me many times for this procedure, which I have followed on many occasions.

As I mentioned, I was helping Don José María when my mistress, compelled by such praise, came to inform me, affectionately, about the decision she had made. I listened to her rather

la oí con tibieza pues se me nublaba el corazón al considerar que iba de nuevo a unos lugares tan memorables y tristes para mí. No estaba el señor enteramente bueno y seguía en cama, pero nos fuimos sin tardanza a la casa de la señora condesa de Buenavista, su hermana, para partir en algunos días. No debía ir yo más donde mis otros señores, pero a pesar de esta orden, fui a despedirme de ellos. El señor don Nicolás, que desde bien chico me quería, con mis servicios me lo había acabado de ganar. Este y su reciente esposa se despidieron de mí llorando y me regalaron con oro a cual más. La señorita me dio unos cuantos pañuelos de holán usados y dos doblones de a cuatro, y mi señor me dio toda la ropa, entre ella las dos casacas que me había mandado hacer y un doblón de a cuatro.

Me despedí de toda la familia y todos llorábamos, pues vivíamos en la más perfecta unión. Me fui tan contrito y entre tantas reflexiones que por la mañana entre nueve y diez, me determiné a pedir papel para buscar amo.[40] Se asombró mi señora de esto. Me dijo que si yo no conocía mi bien y que si ella me llevaba era porque lo debía de hacer, pues no debía de estar sino a su lado hasta que determinara de mí. Me volvió la espalda y sentí haberle dado aquella molestia.

A la hora de la comida en casa de la señora condesa, movió la especie en la mesa manifestando a su hermana mi arrojo y se acaloró tanto que me dijo delante de todos que así era como yo correspondía a los desvelos que había puesto en mi educación. Me preguntó si me había puesto alguna vez la mano encima y por poco lo echo a perder todo, pero dije que no. Me preguntó si me acordaba de la mamá mía y le dije que sí. "Pues yo he quedado en su lugar, ¿me oyes?," me dijo.

Concluido el rezo de por la tarde me llamó a solas la señora condesa en unión de la señora doña Mariana Pizarro para desimpresionarme, creyendo que mis otros amos me habían aconsejado. Les hice saber que temía a mi señora por su genio

---

40. Documento que los amos tenían el derecho de conceder al esclavo que deseaba colocarse o buscar trabajo fuera de la casa de los dueños (*Pichardo novísimo*).

coolly because my heart sank upon contemplating a return to a place so unforgettable and sad for me. The gentleman was not entirely well and was bedridden, but without delay we went to the home of my mistress's sister, the Countess of Buenavista, in order to leave from there in a few days. I was not supposed to return to my other masters' home, but despite that order I went to say good-bye to them. My many years of service had ended up winning over Don Nicolás, who loved me from early childhood. He and his new wife said good-bye to me, weeping, and both heaped upon me generous gifts of gold pieces. My mistress gave me some used batiste handkerchiefs and two four-peso doubloons, and my master gave me all my clothes, including the two coats he had ordered made for me, and one four-peso doubloon.

I said my farewells to all the family and we all cried, for we had lived in the most perfect harmony. I went away so contrite, thinking about so many things, that between nine and ten in the morning I decided to ask for the papers to solicit a master.[33] My mistress was surprised by this. She told me that I did not know what was good for me and that if she was taking me with her it was because she had to do so since I should not be anywhere but at her side until she made up her mind about me. She turned her back on me, and I was sorry for having bothered her in such a way.

At mealtime in the countess's house, at the table she brought up the issue, demonstrating my boldness to her sister, and she became so angry that, in front of everyone, she told me that this was how I repaid all the pains she had taken to educate me. When she asked me if she had ever laid a hand on me, I was about to ruin everything but instead said "No." She asked me if I remembered my mom, and I replied that I did. "Well," she said to me, "I have taken her place. Do you hear me?"

Following afternoon prayers, the countess called me aside with Doña Mariana Pizarro to disabuse me, believing that my other masters had advised me. I let them know that I feared my mistress for her volatile temper, but I could not convince them

---

33. A document that an owner had the right to give to the slave who wanted to place himself or to seek work outside the owner's house (*Pichardo novísimo*).

vivo, pero nada bastó, siempre quedando en su error. Me dijo la señora condesa que yo debía de estar con mi ama y esperar de ella mi libertad.[41]

Partimos por fin para Matanzas haciendo mansión en el Molino. Se me señalaron obligaciones y en poco tiempo me hallé al frente de los que me vieron nacer. De tal modo, que los obscurecía sobresaliendo en mi servicio. Se les daba en rostro cuando tenían algún descuido con la exactitud con que llenaba mis deberes. Esto me trajo gran ojeriza de los demás. En este tiempo ya yo andaba por toda la casa, pero concluido el almuerzo, iba a mis acostumbrados lugares donde cosía de todo.

En esta época nos fuimos a vivir al pueblo en la calle del Río, en casa del señor don Félix Quintero. Estábamos allí hacía cosa de dos semanas, cuando una mañana muy temprano se vino al comedor contiguo al dormitorio de mi señora un gallo fino y cantó. Yo dormía en este lugar. Si el gallo cantó más de una vez no lo sé, pero cuando lo oí, desperté, lo espanté y me puse en pie. A la hora de costumbre se levantó mi señora. Esto fue motivo para que si no hubiera buscado con tiempo al señor don Tomás Gener por padrino, hubiera ido a aprender a madrugar al Molino.

Yo tenía como diez y nueve años de edad y tenía cierto orgullito en saber cumplir con mis obligaciones. No me gustaba me mandasen a hacer las cosas dos veces ni que me abochornaran por trivialidades.

Pero el prurito de abatir el amor propio del que está más cerca de la gracia de su amo es un mal contagioso que hay en todas las casas grandes. Así sucedió que por una de estas razones quiso uno abatirme, ajándome con malas expresiones hasta llegar a decirme la tal de mi madre. Se la volví con otra de igual tamaño. Me dio una gaznatada que no pude evitar, y le embestí. La señora no estaba en casa y yo debía ir a buscarla a las diez en casa de la señora Gómez. Partí antes de tiempo y cuando tornamos a casa se lo contaron. Me interrogó en este asunto y me disculpé diciendo, "El que me dice la tal de su madre está enemistado conmigo."

---

41. Ahora me acuerdo que el pasaje del geranio donato fue después de esto, estando en El Molino. Fue cuando mi madre presentó el dinero para mi libertad y murió tres meses después de aire perlático (nota de Manzano).

for, in their eyes, I was wrong. The countess told me that I ought to be with my mistress and await my freedom from her.[34]

We finally left for Matanzas, with a stop in El Molino. My duties were described to me, and shortly I found myself at the head of those who had witnessed my birth, in such a way that I eclipsed them with my outstanding service. When they were careless, the precision with which I fulfilled my duties was thrown up to them. This brought upon me the ill will of the others. At the time I already had the run of the house, but after lunch I would go to my habitual places where I used to sew everything.

During this period of time we went to live in town on River Street, at the home of Don Félix Quintero. We had been there about two weeks when one morning, very early, a fine specimen of a rooster came into the dining room next to my mistress's bedroom and crowed. I used to sleep there. I do not know if the rooster crowed more than one time, but when I heard it I woke up, scared it off, and got out of bed. My mistress awoke at the usual time. Had I not gone in time to ask Don Tomás Gener to protect me, this episode would have been reason enough for me to have been sent to learn how to get up early at El Molino.

I was about nineteen years old and took a certain pride in knowing how to fulfill my duties. I did not like to be told twice to do something or to be shamed for trivialities.

But the urge to destroy the self-esteem of the one whom the master favors is a contagious evil that exists in all the mansions. And so it happened that for just that reason, someone wanted to take me down a few notches by tarnishing my name with unfavorable statements and even insulting my mother's honor to my face. I returned his insult with an equally severe one. He threw a punch I could not avoid and I attacked him. The mistress was not at home, and I was supposed to pick her up at ten at Señora Gómez's house. I went early, and when we returned home they told her about it. She questioned me about the affair and I begged her forgiveness, saying, "Whoever insults my mother is my enemy." "And so if he does it again, you will

---

34. "Now I remember that the episode about the geranium was after this, when I was at El Molino. It was when my mother offered the money for my freedom and died three months later from palsy" (Manzano's note).

"Conque si te lo vuelve a decir volverás a faltar al respeto de mi casa." Le dije que no faltaría al respeto siempre que no me dijese tal expresión.

Al tercer o cuarto día fuimos a almorzar al Molino. Yo no estaba tranquilo esperando la hora de quiebra. Yo conocía las varias actitudes de mi vida y no dudaba de lo que me iba a suceder. Vi venir al mayoral y no tenía el ánimo ya para aguantar azotes. Me escapé por la espalda del jardín y corrí tanto y en tan breve tiempo que cuando me buscaban por toda la casa yo estaba oculto entre los mangles, camino del castillo. Por la tarde me fui al pueblo a casa del señor conde de Jibacoa, que me apadrinaba. Me daban vergüenza estos apadrinamientos. No estaba a gusto y lloraba a mares cuando me acordaba de la estimación que gozaba con mis otros amos en La Habana. Me afligía más la larga distancia que me separaba de ellos.

No pasaron cinco días sin que, qué sé yo por qué nimiedad, se me mandó buscar con un comisionado. Me ató en la sala y me condujo a la cárcel pública a las once del día. A las cuatro vino un mozo blanco de campo, me pidió, me sacaron, se me vistió una muda de cañamazo, me quitaron los zapatos y allí mismo me pelaron. Con una soga nueva de henequén me ató los brazos y salimos por delante para el Molino. Yo que había olvidado todo lo pasado, probando las delicias de unos amos jóvenes y amables, algún tanto envanecido con los favores prodigados a mis habilidades y algo alocado también con el aire cortesano que había tomado en la ciudad sirviendo a personas que me recompensaban siempre y me veía tratado de este modo, pensé incesantemente que en La Habana lograría mejor fortuna.

Llegué, pues, al Molino. Don Saturnino Carrías, joven europeo, era administrador entonces. Me examinó acerca de la culpa que tenía por aquello. Se lo dije y me mandó al campo sin ponerme la mano encima y sin prisiones. Estuve allí como nueve días en los trabajos de la finca hasta una mañana en que vino mi señora a almorzar y se me mandó buscar. Me vistió de ropa fina y me condujo detrás de la volante otra vez al pueblo. A su servicio ya era yo un objeto conocido por el chinito[42] o el mulatico de la

42. *Chinito.* De "chino": "El hijo o hija de Mulato y Negra o viceversa" (*Pichardo novísimo*).

again show disrespect for my house." I told her that I would not show disrespect as long as he did not repeat the insult.

Three or four days later we went to have lunch at El Molino. I was anxious waiting for the storm to break. I knew the vicissitudes of my life and did not doubt what was about to happen to me. I saw the overseer coming and no longer had the spirit to withstand lashes. I escaped through the back of the garden and ran so much and in such a short time that, while they were searching for me all over the house, I was hiding among the mangroves on the road to the castle. That afternoon I went to town to the home of the Count of Jibacoa, who protected me. Having all these defenders embarrassed me. I did not feel comfortable and cried buckets when I remembered the esteem I enjoyed with my other masters in Havana. The great distance that separated us made me suffer even more.

Five days had not gone by when, for I do not know what tiny detail, a deputy was sent to look for me. He tied me up in the parlor and led me to the public jail at eleven o'clock in the morning. At four, a white country lad came to ask for me; they took me out, dressed me in a burlap outfit, took off my shoes and, right there, they shaved my head. With a new henequen rope, he tied my arms and we set out for El Molino. I, who had forgotten the past, sampling the joys of young and amiable masters, somewhat smug from the favors heaped upon me for my abilities, a bit beguiled, too, by the noble atmosphere I had experienced in the city serving people who always compensated me, and seeing myself treated in this fashion, thought incessantly that in Havana I would have a better chance.

And so I arrived at El Molino. Don Saturnino Carrías, a young European, was the administrator then. He asked me about my guilt in the aforementioned incident. I told him about it, and he sent me to the fields without striking or shackling me. I was there working on the plantation for about nine days until one morning when my mistress came to eat lunch and sent for me. She dressed me in fine clothes and took me to town again, seated behind the coachman. In her service I was already an

María. Todos me preguntaban qué había sido, y me abochornaba satisfacer a tanto curioso.

En estos tiempos fue a la casa la esposa del señor Apodaca, gobernador de La Habana, y se le preparó una función digna del personaje que era.

El pintor y maquinista, señor Aparicio, fue conducido a Matanzas por horas para trabajar la transformación de un escaparate viejo en una hermosa cascada. Debía pintarse algunos emblemas alusivos a la rosa, pues se llamaba la señora, doña Rosa Gastón. Yo le ayudé y concluida la obra me regaló media onza. Ayudándole una noche por gusto a llenar varias guirnaldas, descubrió que le podía ser útil y con poco que le dije, me pidió a mi señora no como oficial sino como peón. Yo le sombreaba en particular las rosas. Por la variedad de formas se conocía que era diestro en este arte. Al retirarse me dio media onza y concluida la función fui gratificado como los demás con un doblón de a dos pesos.

Yo guardaba este dinero con intenciones de gastarlo en La Habana. Pero en esto descubrió mi ama que desde la media noche hasta el día, se descamisaban los criados en un almacén jugando a monte.[43] Yo nada sabía de esto porque ni dormía allí ni se dejaban tampoco ver de mí. Esto era a puertas cerradas.

La primera diligencia de mi señora fue registrarme al día siguiente y hallándome con más dinero del que me había dado me juzgó cómplice. Me quitó todo el dinero, aunque le declaré cómo lo había obtenido. Según ella debía de habérselo dicho y fui otra vez al Molino. Tampoco me sucedió nada a pesar de las recomendaciones. A los siete u ocho días se me mandó buscar.

Transcurrió algún tiempo sin la menor novedad cuando aconteció la muerte casi súbita de mi madre que se privó y nada pudo declarar. A los cuatro días de este caso lo supe. Le tributé como hijo y amante cuanto sentimiento se puede considerar.

---

43. Juego de naipes.

object known as the little half-caste,[35] or María's little mulatto. Everyone asked me what had happened, and I was ashamed to satisfy their curiosity.

In those days the wife of Señor Apodaca, governor of Havana, visited the house, and a reception fit for such an important figure was prepared.

The painter and set designer, Señor Aparicio, was brought to Matanzas for hours to transform an old glass display case into a beautiful cascade. He was to paint some representations of the rose, for the woman's name was Doña Rosa Gastón. I helped him, and when the work was completed he gave me half an *onza*.[36] For my own gratification, one night I was helping him decorate several wreaths, and he discovered that I could be useful to him. With the little I told him, he asked my mistress if I could work for him as an unskilled worker, not as a craftsman. Above all, I shaded in his roses. From the variety of shapes, it was evident that he was skilled in that art. Before he left, he gave me half an onza, and after the reception I was recompensed, like everyone else, with a two-peso doubloon.

I was saving this money, intending to spend it in Havana. But at that time my mistress found out that from midnight to dawn, the servants were losing their shirts playing *monte*[37] in a warehouse. I knew nothing of this because I did not sleep there, nor did they let me see them playing. It was a closed-door affair.

The next day my mistress's first piece of business was to search me, and, finding on me more money than she had given me, she judged me an accomplice. She took away all my money, even though I told her how I had obtained it. According to her, I should have told her about it, and again I was sent to El Molino. Again nothing happened to me, in spite of the recommendations. I was sent for after seven or eight days.

Some time passed without the slightest incident when suddenly my mother, who had lost consciousness, died leaving no testament. I found out about it four days later. As her son and one who loved her, I showed her every possible emotion that

---

35. "Chinito": from "chino," the son or daughter of a mulatto man and a black woman, or vice versa (*Pichardo novísimo*).
36. A unit of monetary exchange.
37. A card game.

Entonces mi señora me dio tres pesos para las misas del alma o de San Gregorio. Se las mandé decir al padre coadjutor. Algunos días después me mandó mi señora al Molino para que recogiese lo que mi madre había dejado. Di al administrador una esquela con la que me entregó la llave de su casa en la cual sólo hallé una caja grande muy antigua, pero vacía. Tenía esta caja un secreto que yo conocía. Hice saltar el resorte y hallé en su hueco algunas joyas de oro fino. Entre ellas las de más mérito eran tres manillones antiguos de cerca de tres dedos de ancho y muy gruesas, dos rosarios, uno todo de oro y otro de oro y coral, pero rotos y muy sucios. Hallé también un lío de papeles que testificaban varias deudas. Había entre ellos uno de doscientos y pico de pesos y otro de cuatrocientos y tantos pesos. Estos debían cobrarse a mi señora y después de éstos otra porción de menores cantidades.

Cuando yo nací, me dedicó mi abuelo desde el campo una potranca baya de raza fina y de ésta nacieron cinco que mi padre iba dedicando a cada uno de mis hermanos. Ellas parieron a su vez y vino a haber el número de ocho. Entre éstas una era deforme y parecía un caballo. Era rosilla oscura y siempre parecía que tenía el pelo untado de aceite por lo que el señor don Francisco Pineda la quiso comprar, pero parece que mi padre pedía demasiado por ella. Esta y otra se malograron en el servicio de la hacienda cargando baúles a La Habana estando para parir. De éstas había los recibos o pagarés.

Llegado el día siguiente di cuenta a mi ama de lo que había y también de los recibos o papeletas. Pasados seis o más días pregunté a mi señora si había su merced revisado los papeles que le había entregado. Me contestó en tono agradable que todavía no. Di esta respuesta a la parda Rosa Brindis que cuidaba de la educación de mi hermana María del Rosario. Como María del Rosario era libre la tenía ella a instancias de mi señora mientras no fuera capaz de gobernarse. Rosa me instaba a que no dejase de recordarle a mi señora cada vez que pudiese, pues quería la parte de mi hermana para su manutención, pues la había criado. Ella sabía que la señora le tenía guardado a mi madre dinero para que lo compartiese entre todos sus hijos si ella muriese. Y yo, como mayor de todos, debía de echar a andar esto. Con tal aviso, cuando pasados algunos días más, aguijado sin cesar por esta mujer, me

one can imagine. Then my mistress gave me three pesos to say mass for her soul, the San Gregorio masses. I asked the assistant priest to say the masses. A few days later, my mistress sent me to El Molino to gather up what my mother had left behind. I gave the administrator a note and he handed me the key to her house, in which I found only a very old but empty box. This box held a secret that I knew. I popped the spring and found some fine gold jewelry in the hollow. Among them, the most valuable ones were three old bracelets, each nearly three fingers wide and very thick, and two rosaries, one made of solid gold and the other of gold and coral, although broken and very dirty. I also found a mess of papers that recorded various debts. There were among them one for a little more than two hundred pesos and another for some four hundred. These debts were to have been collected from my mistress, and besides these there was another batch for smaller amounts.

When I was born my grandfather set aside for me a well-bred bay mare from the countryside, and she produced five colts that my father later set aside for each of my siblings. Those reproduced in turn, and we ended up with a total of eight. Among them, one was deformed and looked like a stallion. She was reddish brown and always looked as if she had been rubbed down with oil, so that Don Francisco Pineda wanted to buy her; but it seems that my father was asking too much. This one and another died in the service of the plantation, carrying trunks to Havana while they were pregnant. For these there were receipts or promissory notes.

The next day I gave an accounting to my mistress of what there was and also of the receipts and papers. After six days or more, I asked my mistress if she had gone over the papers I had given her. She answered, amicably, that she had not yet done so. I reported this answer to the mulatta, Rosa Brindis, who was in charge of educating my sister, María del Rosario. Since María del Rosario was free, my mistress had placed her with the mulatta until she was of age. Rosa urged me, whenever possible, not to let my mistress forget, for she had raised my sister and therefore wanted the portion that rightfully belonged to her for her support. She knew that my mistress had put away my mother's money so that when she died the mistress would distribute it among the

determiné a hablar con mi señora por segunda vez, lleno de las más halagüeñas esperanzas.

Cuál sería mi asombro cuando, incómoda, me respondió mi señora, "¿Estás muy apurado por la herencia? ¿No sabes que soy heredera forzosa de mis esclavos?[44] En cuanto vuelvas a hablar de la herencia te pongo donde no veas el sol ni la luna. Marcha a limpiar las caobas."

Esta escena pasó en la sala del señor don Félix Quintero, serían las once de la mañana. Al día siguiente manifesté a Rosa lo que había pasado. No me acuerdo de todo lo que dijo, sólo que todas sus duras expresiones iban a caer sobre las cenizas de mi pobre madre.

De allí a dos días, eran algo más de las doce cuando apareció, pidió permiso para hablar a mi señora y cuando se le concedió estuvo con ella largo rato. Yo estaba en la despensa que estaba frente a la puerta de la calle haciendo qué sé yo qué, cuando entró la Rosa. Me dijo que fuera por su casa cuando tuviese ocasión. La hice esperar y le di dos de las tres manillas quedándome con una. También le di todos los pedazos de rosarios y un relicario que dicen que en su tiempo no se conseguía ni por una onza. Era grande, guarnecido de cordones de oro, láminas del mismo metal y el divino rostro de Jesús estaba en el medio. Era muy abultado y tenía como dos cuartas de una cadenita muy curiosamente trabajada todo de oro. La envolvió bien, mas estando para partir, mi ama, que no me perdía nunca de vista, se acercó a nosotros y manifestándole no era de su agrado tuviese aquella familiaridad conmigo ni con ninguno de sus esclavos, se concluyó con que ella no volvería a poner sus pies en casa.

Por lo que toca a mí, desde el momento en que perdí la halagüeña ilusión de mi esperanza ya no era un esclavo fiel. Me convertí de manso cordero en la criatura más despreciable. No quería ver a nadie que me hablase sobre esta materia. Quisiera

44. Fernando Ortiz en *Los negros esclavos,* cita a la Condesa de Merlín, quien observa que "aunque el esclavo posee el derecho de propiedad, a su muerte sus bienes pertenecen a su amo." Pero la condesa agrega esta nota benévola: "pero si deja hijos nunca el propietario de Cuba se aprovecha de esta herencia" (p. 315).

children. And I, as the eldest, should set in motion this process. Keeping such advice in mind, after a few days went by, spurred on incessantly by this woman and with high hopes, I decided to speak to my mistress for a second time.

How surprised I was when my mistress, greatly agitated, answered me, "Are you in a big hurry for your inheritance? Don't you know that I am the automatic heir of my slaves?[38] If you as much as speak of the inheritance again, I will put you where you will see neither sunlight nor moonlight. Go clean the mahogany furniture."

This scene occurred in Don Félix Quintero's parlor at about eleven in the morning. The next day I told Rosa what had happened. I do not remember everything she said, only that all her harsh words were to fall upon the ashes of my poor mother.

Two days later at about noon when Rosa showed up at the house, she asked permission to speak to my mistress, and after it was granted she was with her for a long time. I was in the pantry, which faced the front door, doing I remember not what, when Rosa came in. She told me to come to her house as soon as I had a chance. I asked her to wait and gave her two of the three bracelets, keeping one for myself. I also gave her all the rosary pieces and a reliquary, which they say was worth more than an onza when it was new. It was large, trimmed with gold-braid engravings of that same metal, and had the divine face of Jesus in the middle. It was very bulky and very curiously fashioned in gold, with a fine chain, which was some two hand-lengths long. She wrapped it up well, but as she was about to leave, my mistress, who never let me out of her sight, approached us, and, showing Rosa that it was not to her liking that she be so familiar with me or with any of her slaves, she concluded that the mulatta would never again set foot in that house.

As for me, from the moment I lost the illusion of my hoped-for freedom, I was no longer a faithful slave. I was transformed from a meek lamb into the most despicable creature. I did not want to see anyone who would speak to me about this

---

38. In *Los negros esclavos*, Ortiz quotes from the Countess of Merlín, who observes that "although the slave possesses the right to property, upon his death his possessions belong to his owner." But the countess adds this benevolent note: "But if children are involved, the Cuban landowner never takes advantage of this inheritance" (315).

haber tenido alas para desaparecer trasplantándome a La Habana. Se me embotaron todos los sentimientos de gratitud y sólo meditaba en mi fuga.

Pasados algunos días vendí a un platero la manilla. Me dio siete pesos y algunos reales por ella. Y en la noche cuando dejé a mi ama en casa de los señores Gómez le llevé los pesos al padre coadjutor para misas por mi madre. Los reales fueron para velas para las ánimas. No tardó mucho tiempo mi señora en saber por el mismo padre que había mandado decir tantas misas. Me preguntó de dónde tenía ese dinero. Mas como lo que yo menos apreciaba por entonces era vivir, le dije sin rodeos que había vendido una manilla. Quiso saber a quién, mas como di palabra al platero de no decirlo, me sostuve diciendo que a uno que no conocía. "Pues ahora sabrás para qué naciste," me dijo. "Tú no puedes disponer de nada sin mi consentimiento." Fui preso al Molino. Ya era ésta la tercera vez.

Me preguntó don Saturnino lo que había. Se lo dije todo con enfado. La desesperación había ocupado el lugar de todos mis sentimientos. Mi madre era lo único que allí tenía y ésa no existía. Mis lágrimas corrían en abundancia mientras contaba a don Saturnino la distribución del dinero. Me mandó desatar y me mandó para su cocina encargándome no saliese de allí. Me daba de lo que él comía y dormía en el pesebre de los caballos. Me enseñó la carta de recomendación y a la verdad que me hubiera pesado toda la vida la licencia que me tomé.

Pero yo, criado en la oscuridad de tanta ignorancia, ¿qué podía saber? Al cabo de ocho o diez días me llamó y me hizo poner unas prisiones porque venía la señora a almorzar al día siguiente. Me mandó al campo encargándome si me preguntaban si había sufrido azotes que dijese que sí.

A las nueve poco más o menos recibió orden el contramayoral de enviarme para la casa de vivienda. Me resistí a ir, pero amenazado con dureza tuve por buen partido obedecer al administrador que me recibió con una muda de ropa fina de color, eso es pantalones y chupa que vestí. Cuando le fui a entregar aquellos andrajosos despojos me dijo con cierto aire de firmeza estas palabras que me aterraron, "¿Sabes lo que te digo? En menos de dos meses has venido a mi poder en tres

matter. I wished to possess wings so as to disappear, transported to Havana. All my feelings of gratitude were weakened, and I thought only about fleeing.

A few days later I sold the bracelet to a silversmith. He gave me seven pesos and some reales for it. And that night after I left my mistress at the Gómez's house, I took the pesos to the assistant priest for my mother's masses. The reales were for candles for the spirits. It was not long before my mistress found out from the priest himself that I had paid for so many masses. She asked me where I got the money. But since at that time what I least valued was life, I spoke plainly about how I had sold a bracelet. She wanted to know to whom, but because I gave my word of silence to the silversmith, I kept on saying to someone whom I did not know. "Well, now you will find out why you were born," she told me. "You cannot dispose of anything without my consent." I was imprisoned at El Molino. That was already the third time.

Don Saturnino asked what happened. I angrily told him everything. Despair had occupied the place of all my feelings. My mother was the only thing I had there, and she was gone. My tears flowed profusely as I told Don Saturnino about the dispersal of the money. He ordered me untied and sent me to his kitchen, ordering me not to leave that spot. He gave me some of what he was eating, and I slept in the horse stable. He showed me the letter that had accompanied my arrival, and the truth is that I would have suffered the rest of my life for what I had done.

But, raised in the shadow of such ignorance, what could I know? Eight or ten days later he called me and made me put on some shackles, because the mistress was coming for lunch the next day. He sent me to the field, advising me to answer "Yes" if they asked me if I had suffered the lash.

At nine o'clock, more or less, the assistant overseer received an order to send me to the house. I resisted going, but threatened with punishment, I thought it best to obey the administrator, who met me with a change of nice, colorful clothes, that is, pants and a short jacket, which I put on. When I went to give him those tattered rags, with a certain air of assurance, he uttered these words, which terrified me, "Do you understand what I'm saying? In less than two months you have fallen into

ocasiones y nada te ha sucedido. Pon los medios para no volver más porque te llevan los demonios. Anda que la señora te espera. Anda y cuidado."

Este señor, de nacionalidad gallega, era de genio vivo y duro de carácter. Era joven, como de 25 a 28 años y tanto los del campo como los de la casa de vivienda le temían en sumo grado; pues no sólo yo andaba en estos vaivenes.

Cuando llegué a los pies de mi señora me postré y pedí perdón de mi falta. Me mandó sentar en el comedor y acabando de almorzar me mandó un abundante plato que yo no probé. Mi corazón ya no era bueno y La Habana, juntamente con los felices días que en ella gocé, estaban impresos en mi alma. Yo sólo deseaba verme en ella. Notó mi señora el caso que había hecho de la comida y no dejó de maravillarse de que no me alegrase el corazón un buen plato.

Es de admirarse que mi señora no pudiese estar sin mí 10 días seguidos. Así era que mis prisiones jamás pasaban de 11 a 12 días. Siempre me pintaba como el más malo de todos los nacidos en el Molino, de donde decía que era yo criollo. Esto era otro género de mortificación que yo tenía. La amaba a pesar de la dureza con que me trataba. Yo sabía muy bien que estaba bautizado en La Habana.

Otra vez en el pueblo no sé por qué me trata entonces con dulzura. Yo nunca podré olvidar que le debo muchos buenos ratos y una muy distinguida educación. Me mandaba a pasear por la tarde. Sabía que me gustaba la pesca y me mandaba a pescar. Si había maroma[45] también. Por las noches, se ponía en casa de las señoras Gómez la manigua[46] que luego fue monte, y yo debía al momento que se sentaba pararme al espaldar de la silla con los codos abiertos cuidando así que los de pie no se le echasen encima o rozasen con el brazo sus orejas. Cuando acababa, que era por lo regular a las doce o a la una, si ganaba llevaba yo el taleguillo

---

45. Función de volatines.
46. "El juego del *Monte* en pequeño, en casa y personas de confianza, improvisado y sin ceremonias" (*Pichardo novísimo*).

my hands on three occasions, and nothing has happened to you. Do what you can to avoid returning, because all hell will break loose. Get going; the mistress is waiting for you. Get going and watch your step."

This man, a Spaniard from Galicia, had a very hot temper and a harsh demeanor. He was young, about twenty-five to twenty-eight years old, and those in the fields as well as those in the house were extremely afraid of him; for I was not the only one in such difficulties.

When I arrived, I threw myself at the feet of my mistress and begged forgiveness for my offenses. She ordered me to sit in the dining room, and after lunch she sent me a generous plate, which I did not touch. I no longer had my heart in it, and Havana, along with the happy days I enjoyed there, was inscribed on my soul. All I wanted was to be there. My mistress noticed that I had not touched my food and was surprised that a good plate of food did not hearten me.

It is amazing that my mistress could not be without me for more than ten days straight. And so it was that my sentences never lasted more than eleven or twelve days. She always painted me as the worst of those born at El Molino, of which she said I was a native son. This was another kind of mortification for me. I loved her in spite of the harshness with which she treated me. I knew very well that I was baptized in Havana.

Back in town, I do not know why she treated me so sweetly. I will never be able to forget that I owe her many good times and a very respectable education. She used to send me out for a walk during the afternoon. She knew I liked to fish and sent me out fishing. She sent me to acrobat shows,[39] too. At night, at the home of the Señoras Gómez, *manigua*[40] was set up, and later monte, and when my mistress sat down I was to stand behind her chair with my elbows spread open, so that the others who were standing would not crowd her or brush her ear with their arms. When the game was over, which was usually at twelve or one, if she won I would carry the money bag home. When I arrived,

---

39. Performances of dance and acrobatics.
40. The card game of monte when played among friends, in small groups, improvised and without formalities (*Pichardo novísimo*).

para la casa. Cuando llegaba, al recibirlo, metía la mano y cuanto cogía lo daba sin contar.

Le sirvió de mucho asombro y contento cuando me vio haciendo un pantalón por mi cuenta. Lo cosía para el maestro Luna, que tenía su tienda en la casilla que estaba en la plazuela junto a la iglesia. Esta habilidad la aprendí por mí mismo, observando cómo eran los otros pantalones, pues no sabía yo más que costurar túnicas, camisones y guarniciones.

Desde que me llené o me llenaron de la idea de que sería libre pronto, traté de llenarme de muchas habilidades. Ya era repostero y sacaba de mi cabeza muchas ideas a las que favorecía la idea de dibujo que adquirí con los diferentes maestros que enseñaban a los niños. En mis ratos ociosos, que eran pocos, inventaba doblones en pedacitos de papel y luego eran una curiosa servilleta. La flor, la piña, la concha, la charretera, el abanico y otras de menos gracia, son fruto de mis ratos perdidos con ellas. Han lucido algún tiempo y otras lucen aún.

Tenía yo desde bien chico la costumbre de leer cuanto era leíble en mi idioma y cuando iba por la calle siempre andaba recogiendo pedacitos de papel impreso y si estaba en verso hasta no aprenderlo todo de memoria no rezaba.

Así sabía la vida de todos los santos más milagrosos y los versos de sus rezos, los de la novena de San Antonio,[47] los del trisagio,[48] en fin todos los de santos, porque eran los que alcanzaban la mesa de mi señora. En los días de comida, que eran casi diarios, la coronaban regularmente tres o cuatro poetas improvisadores, los que al concluirse la comida me dejaban bastantes versos. Tenía mi cáscara de huevos y mi pluma y apenas acababan mientras otros aplaudían y otros rebosaban la copa, yo detrás de alguna puerta copiaba los trozos que me quedaban en la memoria. Cuando mi ama dulcificó su genio conmigo, yo dejé insensiblemente cierta dureza de corazón que había adquirido desde la última vez que me condenó a la cadena y al trabajo.

47. Rezo dedicado a San Antonio que se practica durante nueve días seguidos.
48. Himno en honor a la Santísima Trinidad, en el cual se repite tres veces la palabra "santo."

upon receiving it, she put her hand in and gave me whatever she grabbed without counting it.

She was very surprised and pleased when she saw me making pants on my own. I was making them for the master craftsman Luna, who had his shop in the stall that was in the plaza next to the church. This skill I learned by myself, observing how other pants were made because I only knew how to sew tunics, chemises, and trim.

Ever since I got or was given the idea that I would soon be free, I tried to teach myself many skills. I was already a pastry cook, and of the many inspirations I had, I favored the idea of drawing, which I acquired from the different teachers who used to instruct the children. In my free time, which was limited, I created doubloons from pieces of paper, which then made a curious little napkin. The flower, the pineapple, the shell, the epaulet, and other less attractive shapes are all fruits of my odd moments spent on them. They were shown off for some time, and others are still displayed.

From early childhood I was in the habit of reading everything legible in my language. And when I walked down the street, I always went along picking up pieces of printed paper, and if it were in verse I would not pray again until I learned it by heart.

That is how I knew the lives of all the most miraculous saints and the verses of their prayers, those of the novena of San Antonio,[41] those of the trisagion,[42] in short, all those of the saints, because they were the ones that reached my mistress's table. On days when there were guests, which was almost daily, normally three or four improvisational poets were invited, and after dinner they would leave more than enough verses for me. Behind some door, I had my eggshell inkwell and my quill, so when they had barely finished, while some applauded and others filled their glasses to overflowing, I would copy the lines that stuck in my memory. When my mistress's temper mellowed toward me, I unconsciously relinquished a certain hardened heart that I had acquired since the last time she condemned me to chains and

---

41. Nine successive days of prayer dedicated to Saint Anthony.
42. Hymn in honor of the Holy Trinity in which the word "holy" is repeated three times.

Como perseveró en no ponerme ni mandarme poner la mano, había olvidado todo lo pasado y la amaba como a madre. No me gustaba oír a los criados motejarla y hubiera acusado a muchos si no me constase que el que iba con un cuento era quien la ofendía. Uno lo hizo donde ella no lo oyó, y el que se lo decía se valía de este medio para molestarla, máxima que le oí repetir muchas veces.

Yo estaba como nunca bien mirado y nada echaba de menos. Me hacía el cargo de que era libre ya, y que se esperaba que supiese trabajar y tuviera edad competente para recibirla.[49] Esto me hizo internarme tanto en ciertas artes mecánicas y lucrativas que si hoy lo fuera no me faltaría ni digo qué comer sino qué tener.

En esta época escribí muchos cuadernos de décimas de pie forzado que vendía. Arriaza, a quien tenía de memoria, era mi guía. La poesía, sin embargo, requiere un objeto a quien dedicarse. El amor regularmente nos inspira. Yo era demasiado inocente y todavía no amaba; por consiguiente, mis composiciones eran frías imitaciones.

Al cabo de tres o cuatro meses de mi último acontecimiento, se armó viaje a Madruga, donde debía mi señora tomar baños. Fuimos en efecto. Con sus males tomó mi señora su antiguo mal humor. Se me echaba en rostro sin cesar la libertad que tomé de disponer de aquellas prendas, habiendo menores que eran en número de cinco,[50] reputando esto un hurto por mi parte. "Vaya a ver en qué manos se pondría la herencia y bienes de los otros, para que lo jugase todo en cuatro días." Sin cesar se me amenazaba con el Molino y don Saturnino. Las últimas expresiones de éste estaban grabadas en mi corazón y yo no tenía la menor gana de volverme a ver con él.

Pregunté cuántas leguas distaba de allí La Habana y supe que doce. Hallé que no las podría vencer en una noche de camino a pie y desistí de pensar más en verme en La Habana. Esperaba que cuando fuese allá mi suerte se decidiría, siempre con la idea de ser libre.

---

49. Es decir, recibir la libertad.
50. Es decir, cinco hermanos.

hard labor. As she persevered in not laying a hand on me or in ordering others to do so, I had forgotten all the past and loved her like my mother. I did not like to hear the servants call her names, and I would have told on several of them if it were not clear to me that he who tattled was the one who offended her, an idea I heard her repeat many times. Someone did just that where she could not hear him, and the one who told her used these very means to annoy her.

I was taken care of better than ever and did not want for anything. They let me know that I was as good as free and only waiting for me to know how to work and be of a competent age to receive it.[43] This made me devote myself so much to certain lucrative mechanical skills that if I were free today I would not lack anything to eat, so to speak, but only possessions.

At that time I wrote many notebooks of décimas, with fixed meter, which I sold. Arriaza, whose poetry I had memorized, was my guide. Poetry, however, must be dedicated to someone. Love provides us with constant inspiration. I was too innocent and did not yet know about love; my compositions were, therefore, cold imitations.

Three or four months after my last incident, a trip was organized to Madruga, where my mistress was to enjoy the baths. We did, in fact, go. Her illnesses made my mistress assume her bad temper of days gone by. She incessantly threw up to me the liberties I took in disposing of that jewelry, when there were five youngsters[44] to remember, deeming this robbery on my part. "Just look in whose hands the inheritance and possessions of others was deposited, so that everything would be squandered in four days." She ceaselessly threatened me with El Molino and Don Saturnino. The latter's final words were etched in my heart, and I did not have the least desire to see him again.

I asked how far away Havana was and learned it was twelve leagues. I discovered that I could not make the trip on foot in one night and stopped thinking anymore about getting to Havana. I hoped that when I arrived there my fate would be decided, always believing this meant freedom.

---

43. Manumission.
44. Five siblings.

Un día, este día de resignación, principio de cuantos bienes y males el mundo me ha dado a probar, es como sigue. Era sábado. Debía, antes del almuerzo, según teníamos de costumbre, asearme ya que vestía dos veces a la semana. Para ello me fui al baño de la paila que estaba al frente de la casa en un declive a unos treinta pasos. Estando bañándome me llamaron por orden de la señora. Ya se puede considerar cómo saldría. Me recibió preguntando qué hacía en el baño. Le contesté que me aseaba para vestir. "¿Con qué licencia lo has hecho?" "Con ninguna," contesté. "¿Y por qué fuiste?" "Para asearme."

Esta escena fue en el comedero[51] o colgadizo de la puerta de calle. Allí mismo mis narices se rompieron y fui para adentro echando dos venas de sangre. Esto me apesadumbró y abochornó, pues a la otra puerta vivía una mulatica de mi edad primera que me inspiró una cosa que yo no conocía. Era una inclinación angelical, un amor como si fuera mi hermana. Yo le regalaba sartas de maravillas de colores[52] que ella recibía dándome algún dulce seco o fruta. Yo le había dicho que era libre y que mi madre había muerto hacía poco.

No bastó lo dicho. Como a las diez me hizo mi ama quitar los zapatos y me pelaron. Aunque esto era muy frecuente, esta vez me sirvió de la mayor mortificación.

Me hizo tomar un barril y me mandó cargase agua para la casa. El arroyo distaba del frente de la casa unos treinta pasos y hacía una bajadita. Cuando llené mi barril me hallé en la necesidad no sólo de vaciarle la mitad, sino también de suplicar a uno que pasaba que me ayudase a echarlo al hombro.

Cuando subía la lomita que había hasta la casa, con el peso del barril y mis fuerzas nada ejercitadas, se me faltó un pie y caí dando en tierra con una rodilla. El barril cayó algo más adelante y rodando me dio en el pecho. Los dos fuimos a parar al arroyo. El barril se inutilizó y se me amenazó con el Molino y

---

51. El original dice en "el comedo o colgadiso puerta de calle." El "comedero" es "el parage de una hacienda de crianza donde acostumbraba comer o pastar un *trozo* de ganado o muchos. Cada *comedero* suele tener su nombre particular" (*Pichardo novísimo*).
52. *Mirabilis jalapa*: planta originaria del Perú, con la flor de diversos colores, que luce por la tarde.

One day, that day of resignation, the beginning of the many good and bad things the world has given me to experience, went as follows. It was Saturday. I was supposed to bathe before lunch, as was customary for us, because twice a week I changed my clothes. So I went to bathe in a large basin located in a gully about thirty paces from the front of the house. While bathing, I was called by order of the mistress. One can only imagine the state I was in. She greeted me, asking what I was doing in the bath. I told her that I was cleaning up to get dressed. "Who gave you permission?" "Nobody," I answered. "So why did you do it?" "To clean up."

This scene took place in the dining room[45] or the front doorway. Right there my nose was bashed in, and I went inside spouting two streams of blood. This grieved and shamed me because next door lived a young mulatta girl about my age who inspired in me unfamiliar feelings. It was an angelic fondness, a love as if she were my sister. I would give her bunches of colorful marvel-of-Peru flowers,[46] which she received, returning the favor with some dry candy or fruit. I had told her that I was free and that my mother had recently died.

What I said was not good enough. At about ten my mistress made me take off my shoes, and they shaved my head. Even though this treatment was very frequent, this time it left me completely mortified.

She made me take a barrel and carry water to the house. The stream was about thirty paces from the front of the house, in a small ravine. When I filled the barrel, I found it necessary not only to dump out half the water but also to beg someone who was passing by to help me hoist it onto my shoulder.

As I was climbing the hill back to the house, with the weight of the barrel and my undisciplined strength, my foot slipped and I fell, smashing my knee against the ground. The barrel fell a little bit in front of me, then rolled back and struck me in the chest. Both the barrel and I ended up in the stream.

---

45. The original says "el comedo o colgadiso puerta de calle." The *comedero* was a place on a breeding ranch where cattle usually ate or grazed. Each such place had its own name.
46. *Mirabilis jalapa:* The four-o'clock flower with fragrant yellow, red, or white flowers that open late in the afternoon.

don Saturnino a quien yo temía. Se suponía aquel suceso como de premeditada intención, y la amenaza era grave. No llegué a la noche sin desgarrar muchos esputos de sangre.

Este tratamiento me mostró de nuevo los errados cálculos que había formado de mi suerte.

Desengañado de que todo era un sueño y que mi padecer se renovaba, me acometió de nuevo la idea de que tenía que verme en La Habana. Al día siguiente, que era domingo, cuando la gente estaba en misa, me llamó un criado libre de la casa y estando a solas con él me dijo, "Hombre, ¿qué, tú no tienes vergüenza de estar pasando tantos trabajos? Cualquier negro bozal está mejor tratado que tú. Un mulatico fino, con tantas habilidades como tú al momento hallará quien lo compre."

Por este estilo me habló mucho rato concluyendo con decirme que si llegaba al tribunal del capitán general y hacía un puntual relato de todo lo que me pasaba, podía salir libre. Me insinuó el camino que de allí venía a La Habana, diciéndome que aprovechara la primera oportunidad y que no fuera bobo. Esto me afligió muchísimo, pues si al menor aviso temía más de lo regular, cuanto más temería con las terribles insinuaciones que me hizo y que no pongo aquí por demasiado impertinentes.

Eran las once de la mañana del día lunes cuando vi llegar a don Saturnino. Se apeó y le tomaron el caballo. Desde el momento en que este señor entró se me acibaró toda la vida. El corazón me latía con incesante agitación y mi sangre toda en un estado de efervescencia no me dejaba sosegar.

Regularmente el lugar común de meditación era mi cuarto. Mientras estaba en él pensaba en alguna cosa con sosiego. Así, estando en él, como a las cuatro, oí que hablaban dos, una hembra y otro criado. Esta era de manos y preguntando aquél a qué vendría el administrador, ésta respondió con viveza, "¿A qué ha de venir? A llevarse a Juan Francisco." Me compadeció aquello y yo quedé enterado de mi mala suerte.

No me es dado pintar mi situación amarguísima en este instante. Un temblor general cundió por todo mi cuerpo y me atacó un dolor de cabeza. Apenas me podía valer. Ya me veía atravesando el pueblo de Madruga como un facineroso, atado,

The barrel was ruined, and I was threatened with El Molino and Don Saturnino, whom I feared. My accident was considered a premeditated plan, and the threat was severe. Before nightfall I had spit up a considerable amount of blood.

This treatment showed me once again that I had been making erroneous suppositions about my fate.

Disillusioned that it was all a dream and that my torment was recurring, the idea that I had to get to Havana again fell upon me. The next day, a Sunday, when everyone was at mass, a free servant of the house called me aside and said, "Look, young man, aren't you ashamed of being so mistreated? Any African is treated better than you. A mulatto youth like you, with as many skills as you have, will find someone to buy him in a second."

He spoke to me in this fashion for a long time, concluding by telling me that if I went before the captain-general's court and told, in detail, about everything I had experienced, I might be freed. He pointed out to me the road that went from there to Havana, telling me to take advantage of the first opportunity and to not be stupid. This worried me very much, because if at the slightest sign of trouble I was unduly fearful, imagine how much more terrified I was by the terrible insinuations that he made to me, too impertinent for me to record here.

It was eleven in the morning on a Monday when I saw Don Saturnino approaching. He dismounted, and they led his horse away. From the moment he entered my whole life was made miserable. My heart beat with incessant upheavals, and my blood, in a state of agitation, did not allow me to keep calm.

My normal place of meditation was my room. There I pondered things calmly. So it was that from there, at about four o'clock, I heard two people talking, a woman and another servant. The former was a handservant, and when she asked the other why the administrator had come, he answered fiercely, "Why do you think he came? To take Juan Francisco away." That made me feel sorry for myself as I found out about my ill fortune.

I cannot begin to paint my very grievous situation at that moment. A general trembling spread throughout my entire body, and I was besieged by a headache. I could barely hold myself up. I could already see myself traversing the town of Madruga like

pelado y vestido de cañamazo cual me vi en Matanzas, sacado de la cárcel pública para ser conducido al Molino.

Recordando las últimas amonestaciones del ya citado don Saturnino, me veía en el Molino sin padres en él, ni aun pariente y en una palabra, mulato entre negros. Mi padre era algo altivo y nunca permitió no sólo corrillos en su casa sino que ninguno de sus hijos jugasen con los negritos de la hacienda. Mi madre vivía con él y sus hijos, por lo que no éramos muy bien queridos.

Todo esto se me presentó a mi alborotada imaginación y en aquel momento determiné mi fuga.

El que me había insinuado el partido que debía de tomar como favorable, a eso de las cinco de la tarde me dijo, "Hombre, saca ese caballo de allí y ponlo allá para que esté al fresco. Allí estará haciendo ruido y despertarán los amos cuando lo vayas a coger para don Saturnino." Al decirme esto me entregó también las espuelas y agregó, "Allí está la silla sin pistolera. Tú sabrás dónde está todo para cuando se necesite." Una mirada suya me convenció de que me hablaba para que aprovechara este momento.

El siempre fue así, muy llevado con mi padre y trataba a mi madre con algún respeto aún después de viuda. No estaba yo con todo esto lo bastante resuelto. Consideraba que dejaba a mis hermanos en el Molino y que tenía que andar toda una noche solo por caminos desconocidos y expuesto a caer en manos de algún comisionado.[53]

Cuál sería mi sorpresa cuando acabando de cenar, y estando yo sentado a solas sobre un trozo meditando si me determinaría o no, vi que don Saturnino se llegaba a mí y me preguntó dónde dormía. Le señalé sobre una barbacoa, pero esto acabó de echar el resto a mi resolución. Tal vez sin esta pregunta no me hubiera determinado nunca ya que yo era muy miedoso. Bien pudo haber sido hecha esta pregunta con toda ignorancia y que todo fuesen habladurías de criados y que todo variase a la hora como en otras ocasiones. Sin embargo, yo no pude recibirla sino

---

53. El esclavo no tenía el derecho de alejarse de la propiedad del amo sin su permiso en forma escrita.

a criminal, tied up, shaven, and dressed in burlap, as I was in Matanzas, taken from the public jail to be led to El Molino.

Remembering the latest threats by the aforementioned Don Saturnino, I saw myself at El Molino, without parents or even relatives, and, in a word, a mulatto among blacks. My father was a bit proud and never allowed small groups in his house or that any of his children play with black children from the plantation. My mother lived with him and his children, which is why we were not very well liked.

All of this ran through my agitated imagination, and at that moment I decided to run away.

At about five in the afternoon, the one who had suggested to me the best decision to take said, "Young man, take that horse from there and put it over there so it can be where it is cool. Over there it will make noise and awaken the masters when you go to fetch it for Don Saturnino." Upon telling me this, he also handed the spurs to me and added, "There is the saddle without holsters. You'll know where everything is for when you need it." His look convinced me that he was talking to me so that I would take advantage of the moment.

He was always this way, friendly with my father and respectful with my mother, even after she was widowed. Even so, I was very much undecided. I thought of how I would be leaving my brothers at El Molino and that I would have to ride the whole night alone on unfamiliar roads, subject to falling into the hands of some deputy.[47]

After finishing supper, I was seated alone on a log contemplating a decision to flee or not to flee when I saw Don Saturnino approaching me; he asked me where I slept. I pointed out a hammock to him, but this was the deciding factor for me. Perhaps without such a question I would never have decided, since I was very fearful. It was possible that this question was asked innocently, that everything was a bunch of servants' rumors, and that later on things would look different, as on other occasions. I could not, however, interpret it except as a very bad

---

47. A slave did not have the right to leave his master's property without written permission.

como de muy mal anuncio en vista de lo que estaba ya en mi conocimiento. Así determiné partir a todo riesgo.

Pensé en la mala suerte de un tío mío que habiendo tomado igual determinación para irse de donde el Sr. don Nicolás, Sr. don Manuel y el señor Marqués, fue traído como todo un cimarrón. Sin embargo, estaba resuelto a echar una suerte y padecer.

Con este motivo velé hasta más de las doce. Aquella noche se recogieron todos temprano por ser noche de invierno y estar algo lluviosa. Ensillé el caballo por primera vez en mi vida. Le puse el freno, pero con tal temblor que no atinaba a derechas con lo que hacía. Acabada esta diligencia me puse de rodillas, me encomendé a los santos de mi devoción, puse el sombrero y monté.

Cuando iba a andar para retirarme de la casa oí una voz que me dijo, "Dios te lleve con bien. Arrea duro." Yo creía que nadie me veía y todos me observaban, pero ninguno se me opuso como supe después. Lo que me sucedió luego lo veremos en la segunda parte que sigue a esta historia.

sign in light of everything else I already knew. And so I decided to leave at whatever cost.

I thought about the bad luck an uncle of mine had when, having made the same decision to run away from Don Nicolás, Don Manuel, and the marquis, he was brought back like a true runaway slave. I was, nevertheless, resolved to try my luck and suffer the consequences.

With this intention, I stayed up until after midnight. That night was a rainy winter's night, so everyone went to bed early. I saddled a horse for the first time in my life. I put the bridle on him, but I was trembling so that I did not manage to do it right. After completing that task, I got on my knees, entrusted myself to the saints of my devotion, put on my hat, and mounted.

As I was about to ride away from the house, I heard a voice that said to me, "God be with you. Hurry along." I thought that nobody had seen me when everyone was watching me; but, as I later discovered, nobody tried to stop me. We shall see what happened to me later in the second part of this story which follows.

VISTE A LOS AMOS } INFRAESTRUCTURA
ASISTE ENFERMOS

———

IMITA EL DIBUJO } MIMETISMO
  LA ESCRITURA
 (LA POESIA)